A LIFELONG JOURNEY

TO WAR AND HOME

EDWARD O. CYR

ISBN 978-1-64468-631-7 (Paperback)
ISBN 978-1-64468-632-4 (Hardcover)
ISBN 978-1-64468-633-1 (Digital)

Covenant Books, Inc.
11661 Hwy 707
Murrells Inlet, SC 29576
www.covenantbooks.com

CHAPTER 1

Warren, Rhode Island, probably its biggest claim to fame is that it's the "smallest town, in the smallest county, in the smallest state." It's where I grew up from 1950s to the early '80s. I'm still there in some respects though, in the old north end of Water Street, known then as the Italian Section. The town around the fifties and early sixties was a typical small New England costal town made up of smaller immigrant ethnic communities. First generation Italian Catholics had settled there, claiming their little piece of America. Other Catholic nationalities also communally carved out their section of Warren. They built and supported their particular church and cultural norms within their section of town. The other non-Catholic religions also did the same in declaring their section within the town. Growing up, I never knew the formal names of any of these churches. In fact, still in present-day discussions, we still refer to them as the Italian, French, Polish, Irish, Portuguese, Baptist, and Protestant Churches. Our north end of town had tight little colonial streets with two-, three-, and the occasional four-story tenement houses. The sea was a vital part of the early economy for Warren in those early colonial years. Some of these homes dated back to the early colonial days of the shipping and boating industry.

In the north end generations of Italian immigrants lived in the same tight area as a general rule, deciding not wanting to leave parents or family or the comfort of the area. A few brave souls moved to other areas of Warren, but the north end was and is and always has been their home. For whatever the reason, it always seemed the Italian grandparents in the north end were always living on the top floor of a family tenement apartment. These tenements housed an array of extended family descendants, sons, daughters, aunts, uncles, and cousins. If they didn't live exactly in the same house, they settled generally close to this area of the town. The old folks, our grandparents, never wanted or saw a reason to move. It seemed to me that this was some sort of unspoken Italian thing, to live in the same house, on the same top floor apartment, for their entire life. I always thought it had to be some badge of Italian heritage honor to be able to claim this fact to St. Peter at the Gates of Heaven. The grandparents all had the same response to moving. They would stay in their house until they died. They would continually tell you this, every day, for the eighty- or ninety-plus years that they were alive. They would also never forget to tell you daily that they were dying, every day, for those same eighty- or ninety-plus years. And when they did die in those days, they wanted some sort of service in their homes. Of course, there were all the relatives from the Providence and Boston area who would arrive to give their condolences. Friends with their kids and anyone else in the neighborhood would also stop by to express their sympathies. And of course there was the food; they always brought food and lots of it. There were so many relatives; you couldn't possibly remember all their names. They certainly couldn't remember yours. For the aunts, it was always a pinch on the cheek, a hug, a squeeze, multiple kisses, and some comment on how big you've grown since the last time they saw you. They seemed to always overdose themselves with too much lipstick and perfume that you couldn't get either of them off you or your clothes. It was the tattoo you wore for the day. They all echoed the same comments. That they'll be next to go and this may be the last time we'll see them. As always punctuating and challenging the other female relatives with this death and dying philosophy as to how they will be the first to go. Who was the sicker, who had the most ills, or who took the most medications. I swear it has to be some type of Italian female hormonal thing. As far as I can remember, the women were always dying, but it was the men who went first. Maybe that was their escape from their wives' constant threat of dying. I guess it was the only way to avoid it, although it was the cheap way out.

There was a certain common neighborhood standard which seemed each household enforced involuntarily. The first and foremost was everyone in the neighborhood grew tomatoes. They grew tomatoes anywhere and everywhere. There were tomatoes in buckets, pots, and small little patches of dirt that paralleled the walkway. For instance, my grandfather, in his later years for instance, had a 1951 Chevy pickup with four flat tires and the truck never moved outside his driveway. But in the bed of that truck during the summer season, there were always five-gallon buckets with tomato plants producing some of the largest tomatoes I can ever remember. Another standard, as I mentioned earlier, was the church. It was integral to this initial generation of immigrants. When they built their cultural Church, it was designed on their European model that bigger was better. If it wasn't bigger, then the Church was given the impression of being bigger, by modeling a big an expansive entry. In order to give this illusion, there had to be about a million stairs to the front doorway with large oak doors. It must have been another unwritten Italian thing in the early years that the Church had to have more stairs than any other. This way the Church looked as if it belonged in Rome and so it had to be a good Italian Church. The downfall to this was if you happened to be chosen as pallbearer for a loved one (which I was a number of times), the casket got heavier with each step. To make matters worse by being heavier, you would always wonder why they had to bury their loved ones with all their jewelry, a countless number of rosary beads, and religious cards. As a youngster, there were so many questions, no good answers, and a slap on the head if you asked why. So you learned, just do, or at least don't get caught not doing!

My grandparents on my mother's side, Emilio and Rosy, owned a corner two-story tenement apartment in which we lived. We lived upstairs, on the second floor across the hall from them. Downstairs, on the first floor, my Aunt Fil, Uncle John, and their three kids were in one apartment. On the other side on the first floor was a small grocery store my grandparents ran for a short while. They evidentially stopped this business and used it as a work area for the stripping of metal for copper, tin, brass, and so forth. This metal stripping was a much more lucrative business, no bookkeeping and not much overhead. My grandmother, a diminutive woman of four feet seven inches, was always fighting the scale. She couldn't understand her weight issue. It always seemed pretty obvious to me. The woman was always cooking, I mean always! Never did I walk into the house that she didn't have a couple of pots on the stove, with something wonderful being prepared. Homemade pasta, bread, fresh vegetables, tomato sauce, heavy with basil, the melding of these aromas and their taste, absolutely marvelous, never to be reproduced. I would be in and out of her apartment all day and always asking, "Eating again, Grandma?" She would always respond that she's "not eating that much and it's only a little bit, just tastes." Of course, it was more than a little bit all day, and it was all the time, every day. I must confess I always also had to have a little "taste." I could never say no to whatever she had on the table, it was always too good and too plentiful to pass up. What used to really demonstrate our generational differences, and I really couldn't get over was when she had the chicken legs sticking out of the saucepan. Claws and all attached and then using the legs as stirring spoons. Slowly cooking and with her stirring until the meat on the legs simply melted off the bone and dissolved into that wonderful sauce.

My grandpa towered over my grandma at a whooping five feet and two inches. Make no mistake; size was not an issue, he was the boss of the family. He arrived in America through Ellis Island from Italy around the beginning of World War I in Europe. He was a baker in the "old country," always pronouncing it "Hit-a-ley." Arriving here in America, Grandpa worked hard, as much as two shifts a day in the Warren mills for six days. He limited his living expenses and helped pay for his brothers and sisters for their passage here to America.

Grandpa never went back to Italy once he left. I would occasionally ask him why and his response never varied. He would always call me boy. He'd say, "Boy, the Italians, they always lose a war, and they don't know how to fight; they switch sides to whoever is winning." Then he would go on a lengthy triad on how the Italians would love, eat, drink, and sometimes get them all confused and do them all together. Grandpa was seventeen when he married Grandma. Grandma was twelve to fourteen years old. Yes, that young, plus she had five younger brothers and sisters, which she was raising. My grandma's family had issues; the best thing to say about

6

my great-grandparents were that they were neither very faithful to each other nor to their children. Yet when Grandpa Emilio married Rosy, he instantly had a family of five siblings, taking in my grandma's brothers and sisters and he raised them all as his own, along with his six children which came later.

Grandma and Grandpa were married for over seventy-five years. You had to laugh when you would visit them later in life and sat in their living room. As they kept reaching each yearly milestone in their marriage, politicians, presidents, and popes would send them congratulatory certificates. Their walls resembled "Who's Who" of influential twenty-century personalities. But these celebrities all died before my grandparents did, and each year, we would put up another plaque from someone new in authority that marveled and celebrated at their longevity together. I can't recall how many times I sat there and commented on the certificates and photos on their wall and those that acknowledged them had died earlier. They were quite proud of these certificates, no matter how yellowed or aged they became. Another interesting note, there was also a tribute to Frank Sinatra and Dean Martin somewhere in the house along with their music at any type of family gatherings.

As I mentioned earlier, our grandparents owned a two-story tenement house with three apartments and a small corner neighborhood convince store. Our potion of the two-story tenement side had two small bedrooms on the second floor, one for my sister, Jackie, and the other for Ma and Dad, while my brother, Armand and I shared the attic bedroom. I say a bedroom with some license, however. It had no heat and no bed. The reason we had no bed was that we were continually fighting and breaking either the mattresses or the bed frames. No matter what our parents did to us, between the jumping and fighting, we broke bed after bed. Finally as a last resort, they put a box spring and mattress on the floor, gave us a couple of large blankets, and that was our bed. It was our bed until I got married at twenty-five years old, in 1976. I went sleeping with my brother in the morning to bedding with my new wife, Patricia, in the evening. The lifestyle on Water Street seemed natural to us: it's the way we grew up; it was the only life we knew. We only had one bureau in which all our clothes fit and we used interchangeably. The only time my brother and I had our own beds were when we were in college as roommates. We did fight at the college. But wisely, we didn't damage the college furniture. There was a damage deposit that we were held responsible for and would have had to relinquish at the end of the semester for any damages that we incurred. Then we would be held accountable to our parents on why we didn't get our deposit back. But on weekends, we would again share the box spring and mattress at home. The older we got, the less fighting we did, and we grew accustomed and comfortable to our sleeping arrangements. As I said, there was no heat, so we would huddle together during the cold winter nights to keep warm, sort of a brotherly spooning. During the summer, it was unbearably hot and pigeons and seagulls would nest in the rafters. I actually learned to communicate with them. To this day, I still boldly think I can confuse them with some of my calls.

My sister, Jacqueline, whom we all called Jackie, was the queen of the house without question; she had one of the small bedrooms in the main portion of the apartment, along with our parents. Fortunately, my sister Jackie was able to have some type of heat during the winter. As previously mentioned, we didn't because not only did our attic not have any heat source heat, but also there was no insulation in the rafters. It was really cold in the winter and really hot in the summer for Armand and me. In the early 1950s, the only source of heat for our apartment was a kerosene heater located in the kitchen. Dad would have to feed the kerosene heater by bringing up from our dirt basement a gallon of kerosene to heat our apartment daily during the cold periods. And as you know, kerosene has a particular order.

These were the little things that meant the passage of growing up. To be allowed to go downstairs into that dirt basement and finally bring up the fuel to heat our apartment. It meant I was getting older and trusted. Simple trusts, but an importance beyond the tasks that maybe our adult parents didn't understand or maybe they really did. Later, Dad was able to change the kerosene heater to a gas heater. We all thought this was safer and it certainly smelled better. Armand and I were not allowed to come downstairs from the cold attic until Jackie was dressed in the morning. As she was the queen of the house, she would dress in front of the heater. But we needed Jackie; we could always count on our sister to sweet talk our parents, especially Dad, to go for a ride in the car and get ice cream or frozen lemonade. My parent's bedroom was small and connected to an overhang of the front hallway. When we frequently didn't have a key to open the apartment door, we would climb the balcony in the main hallway, cross over a banister, walk through my parent's bedroom and into the apartment. Not much security in those days. In fact, although we were surrounded by no less than four to five honest to goodness barrooms, we rarely locked our doors at night. Neighborhood communication was simple and efficient. When my ma wanted me, she would literally open a window, shout my name. If I didn't hear her and come running immediately, anyone in the neighborhood who did hear would relay the message to me that my mother was calling me. On the other side, if Ma chased me around the neighborhood with a broom, which happened more than occasionally, the neighborhood knew that also. Hey, Ma took no mercy on me with that broom, but she very rarely connected. The older ladies would later explain to me why that wasn't proper behavior for a young man. It seemed that within the neighborhood it was common practice for the older ladies to assist in the "proper maturing" of us.

With all things considered, the north end really was a unique place. We would play catch, baseball, football in the street, or handball against the brick wall of our apartment house. I still laugh when I see the commercials replicating this type of childhood experience playing football in the street, such as "go out to Miss Easterbrook's fence, cut across the street to the stop sign, watch for the manhole cover, look both ways, and head out to Union Street, and I'll hit you with the pass." We were able to walk to the neighborhood school, Liberty Street School from kindergarten to fourth grade. We used to go home for lunch, an hour every day. Our mas were always home, no two incomes in those days. Most of the teachers lived in the neighborhood. My first grade teacher, Miss Annie O'Brien and my fourth grade teacher, Miss Rogers, were my Ma's teachers. Miss Rogers actually lived next door, and I discovered later she would update ma all the time on my misadventures. I would find out that there was no escaping the neighborhood watch, their eyes were everywhere, and whatever we did as children was reported to our parents.

There was only one car per most families in those days. We walked everywhere, to Deleckta's, Pharmacy, Jamiel's Shoe World, the grocery stores, such as the A&P and First National, the Lyric Theater, and Woolworths and Newbury's Five and Dime stores. I didn't realize how truly fortunate I was to grow up in that social environment, with those experiences, until I had children of my own. It was a lifestyle in which we would lack economically and yet we never knew financially we were at a disadvantage. It was a lifestyle of simplicity within an uncomplicated living environment. Everyone filled a role within this micro society that was much more clearly defined and accepted in those todays. There was a satisfaction in knowing where we all fit into our family, the neighborhood, our town and our nation as well. Remember, this was post-World War II. All our elders had served in the service, or supported the war, sent their children to war, sacrificed for the war or lost a significant person to the war. Sacrifice and service were expected, it was the norm that everyone shared and understood. It was a time with simple goals and meager means. Yet there was always the believability that we could attain any goal we set our sights on and these goals were all within our reach.

CHAPTER 2

I was the result of two immigrant grandparent families, Italian and French. On the Italian side, Grandma and Grandpa Squillante had six children total, three girls and three boys. The girls all gave them headaches. Each one of the girls had an individual personality, which was very unique. Aunt Fil, the oldest was the most rebellious. My ma, Maria, was the one who didn't want to move away; she wanted to stay connected to her parents and her family until they passed. We did move away once for about a year and half. It was about an eighth of a mile away. Ma cried and cried. Dad couldn't take it any more after a year, so they planned to move us back to Water Street, back to her parents' tenement. Ma was happy, and because she was happy, Dad was very happy and peaceful. The youngest child, Aunt Carrie was the most independent. She was going to tell you what for and when. All their husbands, including my dad didn't dare cross them. I learned that the concept of the man-of-the-house was really not applicable here. The skirts ran the house; the wives were the law, even though the men provided the house. Oh, I'm sure the men had their moments, but the sisters were the owners of each of their families. They also were the loudest; arguments were a common theme between them. Nothing earth shattering. Actually, these arguments weren't really meaningful, just loud disagreements on a regular basis. I actually grew up believing that the arguments and loudness was the normal part of Italian heritage and socialization among siblings.

This was definitely in contrast to my grandparents however. Grandpa was the king, the law, and the enforcer of the family, and that never changed, never! The three boys went in three successful directions. Uncle Pat was a ship builder in the war and later became a janitor for the high school in Barrington, Rhode Island.

Uncle Orlando "Londie" became a family practice physician, later an emergency room doctor for St. Anne's Hospital in Fall River, Massachusetts. Their youngest son, Uncle Emilio, with his education advanced to the position of Chief of Police within the Warren Police Department. This was my Italian side, always very demonstrative. Oh god, the arguments! Lots of explosive discussions, it was a way of life! No one was immune and there were no sides taken. Each of the brothers and sisters were involved and were sucked into these "discussions" at some point in time. But none of the arguments really lasted long, were never really that serious, and never involved the nieces and nephews. The six adult children in the family were always at odds with one or more of the brothers or sisters or maybe the whole bunch. None of us, either the nieces or nephews, ever got involved. As kids, we were immune. No anger was ever directed to us from our adult relatives as a result of these extended family squabbles. We never felt that their love to us was ever dampened due to some ridiculous issue that our parents were temporarily at odds with. Early on, I didn't understand this concept, but as a youth, I recognized it and I appreciated it. The arguments may have been a result of some of our actions, but the aunts and uncles never held back their genuine affection for all of us. Later in life, I appreciated this behavior more and more. This ability to maintain love of family members, while at the same time separating the innocent from the issue, it was an important skill set which we, the grandchildren, learned and lived with from this almost constant family interaction. There was a hierarchy of argumentum standards. Our aunts and uncles did not carry on or extend the arguments into the realm of involving the nieces or nephews. No aunt or uncle ever denied us kids love or affection or food during these "interfamily discussions." The love from my aunts and uncles were something that never was denied from us, no matter what the Squillante brothers and sisters were doing. There was however a good part to this demonstrative attitude. Loud and joyous celebrations were always the usual rule, especially during the holidays and weddings. It was a party anytime the families were together. The energy was constant and most times untamed. It was as if you were in a hurricane, something was always happening or going to happen. If you were in the eye of the hurricane and it was calm, you knew, you just knew something was going to blow in and you just didn't know what the damage was going to be or where it was coming.

My Dad's family, who hailed from Fall River, Massachusetts, was exactly the opposite. My grandfather, Edward Cyr, developed rectal cancer and died in 1949, two years prior to my ma and dad's wedding in 1951. My Memere, Grandma Yvonne, lived for about another thirty-five years as a widower. During the depression, my dad's father was jailed for making moonshine to support his family. My dad would always recount the story of during the depression no one else on the street could afford to have the lights on at night. But Pepere somehow used to illegally tap into the electricity from the neighboring telephone poles to power their house. Oh, he got arrested for that too!

Pepere and Memere had ten children, eight boys and two girls. The uncapped energy on my Italian side was matched by the deliberate and reserved energy of my father's French side. This is not to be confused with not having fun. Uncle Pete was about the craziest and funniest you could be around. Uncle Paul would try to give communion from a fruit bowl after he had filled and personally emptied it with beer. Uncle Raymond was the original long hair, droopy mustached beatnik hippy before there was any. Looking back now, it was probably some form of PTSD from the war. Uncle Louie would play and tell jokes, but his laugh is so hard and endearing that you would join in and not know what you were laughing about. Uncle Tom would help anyone, anytime; your time was his time. If you needed him, he was there for you. Uncle Rich, the only brother who didn't go to war because of his age, was the baby brother. He was quiet, always shaking his head, laughing and wondering how this was his family. The girls, Aunt Pauline and Aunt Anita, were the typical quiet French girls when the family was together, very proper. An uncle I never met was the oldest brother, Uncle Emile. He died in World War II, 82nd airborne, near Mere St. Englse. Uncle Emile was never forgotten, always loved, and never omitted from discussions of the family. The discussions of Uncle Emile always revolved around his dedication to Country, his sacrifice in war, and the effect of his death on the whole family. Because of this, I felt I knew him, although never meeting him. But this side of my family was so different from my Italian side. Seven of these Cyr Brothers, served in World War II. After a few beers, and the laughter began, and their fences down, their war experiences were always shared. That's when I became more reflected; I would listen time and time again, of their same stories, and wonder what type of soldier I would be, or even if I would become one.

Visiting my Memere was, even with all the family present, a more reflective time. She would have her favorite rocker and that was her place. No one sat there, ever, that was her place whether one showed up or the family in its entirely. If family began to talk ill of someone, she would remind them that it was not the proper thing to do, and it would end. When the language began to be less than civil or loud, she would quietly remind her family to stop, and it did. Memere would actually turn red but never raise her voice and gave a quiet direct and deliberate order and it was followed. So when the family began their antics, it was always funnier and more enjoyable. The rules were being broken, and Memere was losing control. She never lost control totally, but the family had taken over, and it was fun to be part of the rebellion.

There were a few things I can truly remember about growing up in this bi-cultural family that always impressed me. The first were all my aunts and uncles, either by blood or marriage, were my aunts and uncles; there was no aunt-in-law or uncle-in-law, and never calling them by their first name. I didn't know that there was a difference between blood and marriage or if there was a difference. As far as I knew then and still do, they are my relatives. One thing about me was true; I was a pain in the ass. I did about everything wrong. I caused trouble wherever I went. I broke things, I caused arguments, I got in people's ways, and I made myself an irritation. I drove my parents nuts most time by cutting my ma and dad's bed post or painted the stove green. But never, never did any one of my aunts and uncles refuse me or not help me. Most times I didn't have to ask, they just did for me. When I did ask, no matter how involved they may have been with other projects, I always felt I was their most important task at that moment. There was a comfort from that kind of love, I probably didn't deserve it, but it was given to me freely by all of them. I didn't realize how valuable, treasured, and lucky that love was until I became older and had to demonstrate it to others in a like manner.

The second strength of this bi-cultural family helped forge me into a career and life commitment direction, which I didn't really realize at the time. It wasn't until I was well along and involved in this military career in which I required my wife and family to sacrifice with me that I understood the impression my relatives had made upon me. It became clearer through my thirty-year plus army military career in the active, reserve forces and deployments. Not one of my father's brothers graduated from high school, and none were officers. Theirs was not some well-established military heritage dating back to the revolution or some Ivy League education. This is in contrast to my mother's family who sent to war a physician, a dental tech, and a ship builder. In addition my mother's sisters' husbands who were enlisted men, who also took pride in their performance of their duties during the war. My father's family gave me a quiet simplicity and an alternate way to define my life while contrasting my mother's more emotional demonstrative side. Both sides of the family singularly gave me strength and purpose to pursue a path of service to Country. They all had the same commitment and belief; this Country will reward you for work and sacrifice. This was ingrained into me without my full knowledge but was the guiding force, which influenced my decisions to serve. They all shared pride in service, pride in Country, pride in sacrifice, and a love of family. They imparted upon me the confidence to strive, the strength to endure, the pride, love, and devotion to continue no matter what the obstacles, and to do it in a quiet low-key manner. How did men who only knew hard honest work give this to me? It was driven into me by their humble devotion to our Country, their Faith, and their families. Sacrifice, service, and loyalty, to both family and Country, these are the values, which were uniquely shared by these two separate families and imparted upon me.

CHAPTER 3

My father was one of seven brothers in World War II. Six were in the army and Uncle Paul the lone Navy man. At family gatherings, I can remember the pride and joy their military experience gave them as they shared wartime experiences. As a "few" drinks were taking hold, the stories they recanted were not of their hardships, but their mishaps and near misses which was followed by laughter and a "how did we ever survive that" type of head shaking. Then my uncles would swap tales detailing their experiences and near misses. My aunts were always there, glancing at them with a look of love in their eyes, but their facial expression of "they will never grow up." Their military service stories either always started with Uncle Emile or somehow evolved to him.

As mentioned, Uncle Emile never came home. He started out as a National Guardsman. The war started and one of his first assignments was in the cavalry. As I understand, he had a restless nature. The 82nd Airborne was new, and he wanted to be part of this new exciting unit. The last time my dad saw him was at home, when they both were on leave from the army. Uncle Emile and Dad were the same size. Dad gave Uncle Emile his military overcoat because Uncle Emile's was not quite up to military standards. Dad was always a little more than attentive to his looks and Uncle Emile was a more disheveled type of person. Since Emile had to leave first, Dad gave him his inspection ready overcoat. That was the last time Dad and Emile was to ever see each other. They missed each other at Fort Campbell by a day prior to Uncle Emile's overseas departure. As we understand, Uncle Emile made the jump into France on D-Day. He was killed a few days later in the hedgerows. He's buried in France at the request of my Mermere. She believed he died with his buddies in the service of his country, and he should remain with them. My Uncle Pete always said that when he saw Uncle Emile in heaven, or wherever, the first thing he was going to do was punch him in the mouth for joining the airborne. Then hug him and tell him how much he missed him all these years and what he missed. Uncle Emile's picture was always in our house in Warren, he was the oldest brother and my dad's best friend. On my Memere's bureau, until the day she died was Uncle Emile's black and white picture in his uniform. The Purple Heart medal, in its contrasting vibrant purple and gold, proudly displayed alongside in the same frame as his picture. Our Country, for her son's dedication and ultimate service and sacrifice, presented the medal to Mermere. As the years rolled on, I began to understand that the losing of a child is the greatest loss. The death of a spouse, parents, and close friends hurt, but when a parent loses their child, part of their soul is lost and the hurt is forever. I understood this common theme more and more as I grew older as I witnessed it a number of times. It is a hard lesson, one I can only pray I will never have to learn.

The Cyr's brother's time in the military always brought some interesting highlights of these young men and their experiences. Dad was a medic, a private first class (PFC), stationed at Walter Reed in Washington, DC. He was released early from the military due to a heart condition. Never wanting to claim a disability, feeling he did what he could for his country and not deserving payment for that service, he never filed a claim. He was assigned to the Section 8 ward. Termed section 8, it was, in those days, the Psychiatric Ward. He escorted many of the soldiers around and tended to their daily needs. He never said a bad word about these guys, always saying they needed the attention not the medications. So he would give a soldier with a headache a white aspirin. If someone had a runny nose, he got a green aspirin, a pain in their arm or legs, a yellow aspirin, a stomachache, then he would get two different colored aspirins, and so forth. Dad would laugh, but he said he never had any issue with the soldiers and they all got better. After he was released from the service, he returned home. Dad took on the elder son responsibility and helped Mermere with Uncle Emile's notice of death in a war zone and was a mentor to his sisters and Uncle Richard, the youngest brother. Dad was Uncle Rich's best man at his wedding years later, and Uncle Rich was Dad's. Dad walked Aunt Pauline down the aisle and proudly gave her away in marriage as both their father and older brother had passed.

Uncle Pete was in the Artillery. In trouble most of the time, he was responsible for most of the trenches being dug for the units' latrine. How else do you discipline someone in a war zone that doesn't really break the rules, just continually bends them? So he was usually tasked to dig sanitation holes all over Europe. As was his custom, Uncle Pete used to sleep in the nude in his sleeping bag. Why I don't know? He never really gave a good explanation why. As is common in war, boredom precedes the craziness of battle. Well, as Uncle Pete tells it, it was the middle of the night and the enemy started some sort of commotion. So his artillery battery was called into action. Uncle Pete was overzealous and responded immediately and began to feed the big guns shell after shell. But Uncle Pete was bone naked, not a stitch of clothes on! The way he told it, after a while, the lieutenant came by and told him to put on some clothes. He didn't listen to him immediately, waiting until the mission was completed. Two things happened after this incident, Uncle Pete was ordered to wear clothes while sleeping and he had to dig another latrine.

Uncle Louie went into France a few days after D-Day; I believe it was D-Day plus 6, as a driver of a two and a half ton truck (called deuce and a half) as part of a transportation unit. There were two primary stories he tells most frequently and laughed louder each time he told them. The first story, they were convoying with a huge line of deuce and a halves. It was late at night, no moon, pretty dark, and they were naturally unfamiliar with the roads or terrain. There was a stonewall with another unit on the other side. So the commander felt that this was a fairly safe place to bed the men and trucks for the night. The guards were placed in their appropriate places and my uncle's unit settled in for the night. Well, at first light, a panic call from the men on guard duty brought my uncle's entire unit to their fighting positions. It appears that the unit on the other side of the stonewall was a German unit, who had bedded down for the night, they believed that my uncle's unit was another German unit. The Nazis didn't realize that they were Americans as my uncle's unit didn't realize they were the enemy, separated by this four-foot stonewall. My uncle then would laugh, that the Nazis were a much smaller unit and more scared than we were and they just surrendered. No shots were fired, just a lot of yelling and confusion on both sides, with neither side understanding the other. But truly, my Uncle Louie's claim to fame is his second story of actually coming face to face with General George Patton. Later in the war, he was in the first deuce and half of a large convoy with a young green second lieutenant. Small narrow roads were the norm in Europe and traffic jams were common. The Nazis had mined the fields bordering the roads as a way to slow the Americans trying to avoid those congestions. Well, Uncle Louie is tooling down the road leading the convoy, the lieutenant reading the map, trying hard not to get lost and trying not to lose either his men or equipment and complete the mission on time. Who do you think they meet up with, the enemy? No, it wasn't the enemy; it was someone more frightening: General George Patton leading his tank convoy. Patton gets out and tells the lieutenant that this is HIS road and he wants the lieutenant's convoy off his road so his tanks can run. The lieutenant tries to explain that it may be dangerous because there were reports that the enemy had mined the fields. Patton then calmly explained to this green lieutenant that if he didn't move this convoy off HIS road, his tanks were going to roll over all the deuce and halves in my uncle's convoy. Uncle Louie said he didn't say a word, he just sat there behind the wheel, this was Patton, and they all believed he was crazy enough to do whatever he said he would do. Well, what did they do? This is where Uncle Louie loses it and laughs harder each time. He said the lieutenant got back in his truck shaking and ordered his whole convoy into the field and they proceed to drive around Patton's tanks. He said they all held their breath hoping the Germans didn't have time to mine the field. The field was unplowed and grassy with minor hills and divots. They were bouncing all around, while Patton's tanks went rambling at top speed down the road. They passed the area cleanly, there were no mines planted, but Uncle had faced General Patton and survived.

Uncle Louie, as my dad, had one regretful story to tell about Uncle Emile. Dad always regretted missing my Uncle Emile by twenty-four hours at Fort Campbell, never seeing him again. Uncle Louie had arrived into France, as I said just days after D-Day. Uncle Louie went through Mer St. Eglise, not knowing that his brother had died in the area. He had helped clear the bodies of fallen soldiers. Uncle Louie always regretted that he had not been able to know that his brother was there. Uncle Louie always felt as if he was so close to touching his brother at that time, he could have prayed over him, taken care of him, and said goodbye to him as a representative of the whole Cyr family. Uncle Louie and his wife, Aunt Joan, confided in me that Uncle Louie, all these many years had still suffered with sleep issues from world war two. He admitted that he would awaken thrashing and punching Aunt Joan in her sleep. His dreams were that he was covered by dead and wounded soldiers, and he was trying to crawl his way out from under them.

Uncle Paul was the Navy man. During the war, he was assigned to the ship, *St. Paul*. He would tell everyone that the ship was named for him. He also was the only brother to be assigned in the south Pacific. He would taunt his brothers with stories of better living conditions, food, and weather than their army in the European theater. He attended and continued with the reunions of the *St. Paul* crew throughout the years. Uncle Paul's ship was attached to the Task Force 38. The St. Paul screened the aircraft carriers when they performed destructive air strikes on Kure, Kobe and the Tokyo areas industrial sites during his tour on board ship. When they decommissioned the ship, he was able to get portions of the deck, which he displayed with his awards. He was proudest that the *St. Paul* was the second ship, which sailed into Tokyo harbor after the surrender. The youngest brother to serve, Uncle Tommy, stayed in the service after the war as a member of the National Guard. Uncle Tom was a cook, actually a very good one considering the equipment he had to work with. He had great pride in being able to serve great food to his troops. At about eighteen years of service, some "new officer" came into the National Guard and tried to tell him how to cook for his men. After cooking for so long in less than ideal conditions, he was too proud to have to take orders from someone "so green." So he quit the service before he was able to earn his retirement. He regretted his impetuous action over and over again, saying he should have just said yes and then do whatever he wanted anyway. This I learned from him about the service, most times, being thick headed only hurts you. Uncle Armand married to my Aunt Pauline, was a career naval reserve sailor. He was too young for World War II and too old for Vietnam. But he served for twenty years and was part of the family's military history.

My ma's part of the family, the Squillante side, also had its military connections. The pride of service during the war from this side of the family was a more reserved experience. The pride of service they related to was more of the sacrifices and horrors of war they witnessed. Through the Squillante side, I was able to see the stupidity of war, but the necessity of war. The youngest son, Uncle Emilio was a member of the Seabee's. He was stationed in Hawaii as a dental tech for most of World War II. Being in the right place at the right time, Uncle Emilio was in a detachment of medics that were assigned to make some of the island landings. But prior to the war, he was enrolled in the University of Rhode Island, majoring in pre-dental. So they yanked him off the landings assignment and assigned him to Hawaii in the dental section. That was a good thing too. Among other difficult war zones, one of the landings was Guadalcanal Canal. Uncle Emilio was extremely lucky, as no one from his initial detachment of medics made it home by the end of the war. These dedicated medics all became causalities of war. While in Hawaii, one of his duties would be to help the oral surgeons reconstruct the jaws of those who were injured in battle. Uncle Emilio was also schooled in the art of pulling teeth after the dentist would administer the local anesthetic. During his time in the dental activity, he made a necklace of teeth. He tells us he always asked the service member if they wanted their teeth. Those that didn't want their teeth, he kept, cleaned, and a fine drill was used for the threading of a chain, which he would wear around the clinic. Quite proud of this, Uncle Emilio intended to bring this back to Rhode Island as a souvenir of his time in the military. Of course, this was a no-go, and he had to surrender his necklace prior to leaving Hawaii. He still lamented over his lost necklace decades later.

Uncle Londie and Uncle Pat really need to be discussed together. Uncle Pat was the oldest child, followed by Uncle Londie. Uncle Londie was really a prodigy. He was thirteen years old and graduated from high school with Uncle Pat in the same year. If you look at their high school yearbook however, you will only see a picture of Uncle Londie. By Uncle Pat's place within the yearbook, you will see, "Photo not available." My grandma Rose was always upset about this, it seems Uncle Pat liked to gamble and he was truant from school that day gambling away the picture money. Both were accepted to College. Uncle Londie was accepted to the University of Rhode Island (URI) after high school. Uncle Pat went to Providence College (PC). The first day at the university, thirteen-year-old Londie was sent home. The school officials thought he was lost and looking for a high school. So Grandma and Grandpa had to go to URI with his diploma and in broken English tell the admission officials that their son earned a spot at the university by graduating high school at age thirteen. I guess reluctantly the officials accepted Uncle Londie into the university. Four years later, Londie was accepted at the University of Maryland Medical School and became a medical doctor at the age of twenty-two. Uncle Pat truly was brilliant in math, understood the analytical concepts and tutored nieces and nephews years later as they went to college, but Uncle Pat matriculated at Providence College for only one year. My grandparents gave Pat his college tuition, money for his transportation to school, and daily packed his lunch. There was only one issue with this whole process; Uncle Pat continued to gamble away all this money. He never attended class for the entire year. He enjoyed gambling daily more than the college scene for a whole year. As you can well expect, this did not really go over big with Italian immigrants who sacrificed for the success of their male children.

Uncle Pat was success in other ways. He was married early, and by the time World War II arrived, he had four daughters (a fifth was born in 1950). Because of his family situation, Uncle Pat was awarded a deferment from the service. To support the war effort, he became a ship builder in a Brockton, Massachusetts, shipyard. His service and duty to his country during wartime came at a huge price. He developed the lung condition asbestosis. As with so many men and women in those days, the dangers of asbestos, which was used routinely at the time, were unheard. He suffered miserably for the rest of his life. Toward the end of his life, oxygen tanks and a severely limited physical ability marked his days. Yet as he got older and Uncle Pat's health continued to decline, he continued to partake in his habit of challenging the odds. He had given his life to our country, not on the battlefield, but as one of the homeland defenders sacrificing their health to manufacture the most powerful navy in the world. His sacrifice and support during the war was as valued, although no medals were ever awarded him.

Uncle Londie was drafted into the army as a general practice physician. In the army his medical unit was sent into the Pacific rather than the European theater. He rose in rank rather rapidly, and by the time he left the army, he was a lieutenant colonel, the highest ranking of my relatives. Uncle Londie was very humble about his military exploits. He had seen much experiencing war at its worst, only occasionally sharing tidbits with family. It was not until much later was I able to relate to his quiet sadness in discussing his experiences of war. Not truly understanding fully until after I had experienced war myself as a health professional in war. I served as an anesthesia provider through three rotations of armed conflict (Kosovo and two in Iraq). Not until you deal with the aftermath of battles do you truly understand the cost of war. The smell of sweat mixed with human waste, blood coagulating, going cold as it leaves the body, sounds of confusion, pleading and pain above the providers' frantic attempts in trying to stop death and dismemberment. The teamwork of organized chaos as numerous health professionals come together, working feverishly for hours upon hours as a team attempting to preserve a life or save a limb. This is the chaotic normalcy of battle's aftermath. Most times, even when there is a somewhat seemingly a successful resuscitation, the outcomes are uncertain as the patients are transferred to the next higher level of care. There is always a feeling of exhaustion. Knowing that causalities, often times multiple ones exceeding the limits of resources available, will be arriving shortly over and over, again and again in a never-ending tide. There never seems to be a shortage of injuries. How do you relate the pain you experience of loss of life and limb of young men and women on an almost daily rate to relatives after you come home? It's not possible; words, no matter how eloquent, can transmit the full experience of pain and horror which you daily witness.

Uncle Londie went ashore on multiple combat island invasion landings with the troops under enemy fire throughout the Pacific. As a physician and first line of health care for the invading troops, he performed immediate life-saving measures while under fire. After the landing site was secured, he was part of the medical team to try to salvage young men. As part of the medical team, they attempted to not only to save the lives of these brave men, but hopefully to prepare them to live their life as best they were able with whatever physical or emotional wounds they received. Even though serving as a general medical practitioner, he was called upon to perform numerous surgical procedures. To the combat troops who served and face death following orders from their superiors, they depended and gambled their life on the medical teams' dedication, ability, and life-saving decision making. Time was and is not a luxury in dealing with the horrific war-inflicted wounds. The medical team's sole purpose is to first combat death. Secondly, the medical team must rob and diminish the destructive powers of war and the insults caused to a service member's body. Uncle Londie's war was one of constant battles against the enemy of death and the destructive powers of war. He had experienced the full spectrum of war on a number of fronts. He was involved in its initial combative invasion force darting bullets, trying to stay alive, and then through a humane attempt to make some sense of wars stupidity. He was called upon to even be part of a health care team administering to the very enemy forces and their peoples who were attempting to destroy him and his fellow Americans. In addition to war's craziness, Uncle Londie's service was rewarded with contracting malaria, and it episodically affected him throughout his life, never allowing him to forget the jungles of the South Pacific.

There were two incidents that resulted from my uncle's service that made an impression upon me. I still to this day vividly relive them. The incidents impacted subliminally on my military career and not until later in my service did I realize how important they were to my development and guidance as a soldier and health care provider. The first still lives with me and pains me to this day. Both of these incidents happened in the late 1950s and I was not quite ten years old. As I said earlier, I was a pain in the ass, not intentionally meaning to hurt anyone; I often said and did things which I would later regret. Always wondering afterward why I said or did such a stupid thing. There was no internet gaming in those late 1950s. No realistic computer-designed graphics. But as a young child, World War II, the Korean War, and the Cold War was so much a part of our lives. For a young child, it had a glamorous effect upon our play-time. We all wanted to be soldiers and war heroes. Hollywood had heroes, movies of Americans doing glorious heroic feats in combat to preserve our sacred way of life. As a young child, sports and war were our games. Either hitting the game-winning home run or being the last man standing against an insurmountable enemy, these were the ambitions of the fifties. Davey Crockett was the hero of the Alamo (in fact, I still sing that song); John Wayne was the man who was the defender of our freedoms and the Lone Ranger and Hop-a-Long Cassidy were the preservers of righteousness. So it seemed natural for me to hear about my uncles and their exploits in the Great War for our freedom. Since my grandma Rose was always next door cooking, I would always bait her for information of her sons at war. She would always tell some interesting tale and allude to uncle Londie as almost not coming home. Never really telling me why, I assumed it was because of the multiple island landings under fire. But one day she did tell me the story. She also told me not to tell anyone that it was a family secret, one the family knows of but never speaks. So now Grandma baited me, what was I to say? Of course I wouldn't say anything. This was a true war story of my family member, a hero, and this was going to better than any movie. So Grandma and I sat at her dining room table and she softly told me a family war secret. Why she whispered, I don't know, it was just she and I.

It was after a battle on one of the islands. Uncle Londie and a friend were walking along a deserted stretch of beach. Uncle Londie had to urinate, to relieve himself. So he left the serenity of the white sands, tropical weather, and crystal blue water to go further inland to relieve himself in privacy. It was unexpected; the area was supposed to be cleared of the enemy. But it wasn't. As Uncle Londie walked alone into the plush overgrowth, a Japanese soldier jumped from one of the trees and attacked him. Remember this was the forties; medical personal had a red cross on their helmets and no weapons. Uncle was alone and unarmed; he had to literally fight for his life, hand to hand. He was wounded and bloodied. It was man against man, life versus death. To live, he had to take the life of another. He was a trained physician; he had taken an oath to preserve life, not to take one. It is a horrible thing to feel life leave someone, to watch him or her take their last breath and feel the cold take over the warmth of their body that signifies life. But he had no choice, he wasn't given one. His future was only to be had by the death of this enemy. I can still see Grandma's eyes heavy, tearing, retelling this story. Her son had survived, wounded and bloodied. He had lived by taking the life of another, something foreign to him. Yes, it was an enemy, and yes, the enemy had not given my uncle a choice. But the man my uncle was, his upbringing and his life's vocation, this was an ironic action. My uncle stumbled out of the brush to his friend on the beach. He was taken to the hospital and treated. He was awarded the Purple Heart and considered a hero. But he didn't see it that way. He was a physician, his job was to heal. He had to be brutal and deadly to survive.

I was young and innocent. To me at the time, it was exciting. How could he be upset at killing the enemy? Why didn't the family want to make this public and make sure everyone knew that Uncle Londie was a hero in combat? After all, this was war, the enemy had a choice, and he could have surrendered. Instead this enemy soldier tried to take out my uncle. This was a combat story out of the movies, and it happened with one of my family members. How could I not tell anyone? I thought, okay so I won't tell anyone, but I can ask Uncle Londie about it, why not? I wanted him to tell me the whole story. How he had overpowered the enemy in hand-to-hand mortal combat and won. How did he kill this enemy? This was the real deal, not some television show or classic Hollywood saga. I wanted the whole story and I was going to ask Uncle Londie directly. Throughout my life, I had seen my uncle Londie in critical life and death situations. He was always calmed, calculating, and direct in an emergency. He would exude confidence in his actions and his decisions. He was the leader in emergency situations with his medical skills. I witnessed so many times the nurses and aides eagerly responding without question, to my uncle's orders during an emergency, having full confidence in his medical judgments. I wasn't prepared for the type of response to my inquiry about this one sole encounter with that enemy.

One day shortly afterward, Uncle Londie was visiting Grandma. He was sitting on the corner of the dining room table. His fedora was still on head, cigar not burning in his mouth, and his black medical bag at his feet. When I heard he was at Grandma's, I left my apartment, ran across the hallway, and entered my grandparents' apartment. We exchanged the usual hellos. I quickly pleaded with Uncle! "Tell me, please, please tell me about the enemy soldier you killed in the war!" As soon as the words left my mouth, I knew I had done wrong and said something I would forever regret. Uncle, as always, was kind and courteous. But Uncle paled, the color from his face drained. His mouth opened in gasp and I thought his cigar would fall. His expression was immediately changed from the gladness to see me to one of startled injury. His air of confidence was instantly transformed into confusion and hurt. He was speechless, his whole body drooped, and his eyes gazed downward. For a moment, Uncle's mouth moved, but no words came forth. I knew at that moment I did a bad thing. I made a mistake and I couldn't take it back. I hurt him, I truly didn't mean too, but I did. At the time I really didn't know why, but I knew I had crossed some line. Finally some words mumbled out. From what I remember, he nodded, said something about yes, it was true, but it was something he would rather not talk about. Even then at my young age, I knew I had done something wrong to terribly hurt him, I was uncomfortable and I had to leave. I remember excusing myself, returning to my apartment, and vowing never to bring the topic up again. At that moment, I realized what my uncle's priorities were, what he had dedicated his life too and how that incident was a reminder to him of the ironies of life. In my youthful excitement and innocence of war, I had crossed a line of honor to respect the wishes of a family member about a memory he wished to suppress. Uncle Londie had taken no great honor in defeating the enemy, no joy in killing another person, even at the cost of possibly losing his own. Never again did I ever talk of this to him. This was one of my first indications that war has costs and hurts that never subside or leave. The war experience becomes a part of your very being. War, in some way or another, forever contributes to the uniqueness of your identity and how you define yourself, and no matter how one tries to bury its impact, war's horrors could be relived and triggered by even the innocent questioning of an exuberant young boy.

The other incident I can remember about Uncle Londie's experience was a much happier moment in time in the late 1950s. My Uncle Londie was asked to be the Parade Marshall and lead a Veterans' Day parade in Warren. The parade's route was on Water Street, past our house, to its northern end where it merges into Main Street. Once on Main Street, the parade traveled south and passed through the center of town to the Town Common site. Once there, a wreath was placed on a memorial by my uncle, and he spoke a few words about the cost of war. As I mentioned previously, World War II and the Korean War's scars were still open and painful to a Nation, which bleed so much in preserving its democratic way of life. I can never forget my uncle walking down the middle of the street in a white suit, with a blue VA overseas cap on with a cane in his left hand. Two of my cousins, who were cub scouts, flanked him on each side. One was his son Dickie, later a Vietnam vet, the other was his nephew, Teddy, a Vietnam era vet, son of my Aunt Fil. The constant waving, clapping, and shouts of recognition from the spectators with each of his steps were impressive. This type of recognition reinforced my thoughts that these town folks were recognizing his war efforts.

Looking back at this, in truth, the town folk were probably more impressed and appreciated his patient care in tending to their medical needs. I'm sure they understood and recognized his military duty and sacrifice, for they all shared the same hardships of war in one way or another. But hey, they didn't know our family secret of his wartime survival, which I now knew, but wouldn't share. I wanted so much to be marching alongside of my uncle and cousins. I can remember thinking, to be able to walk down a hometown street in a parade with family members, being so loudly recognized as a returning war veteran, had to be the ultimate experience. Longing for that experience is something that has stayed with me my entire life. It was something I felt I would never be able to replicate. As my military profession grew and required more sacrifices of my family, having them share that similar parade experience was something I yearned. To be honored and able to share with them the joy of all of us as a family being recognized as we shared this war-time sacrifice together, marching down main street, was something I never imagined it would ever occur. But it did, by surprise, many years later.

With my return from Iraq in 2003 and 2007, as fate would have it, I, with my wife and family, would be able to march down our hometown, of Bristol, Rhode Island. Bristol, Rhode Island, is the home to the longest, continuous Fourth of July Celebration and Parade in the United States. I was fortunate to be asked to lead the Military Division within the parade on this memorable day in 2008. I proudly marched with my wife, Tricia, with her strength beside me, followed by my five daughters and their husbands and boyfriends at the time, throughout the parade route. The following year, on July 4, 2009, I was asked to be the principle Patriotic Speaker to signal the start of the festival and parade. During these two instances, all I could think of was my Uncle Londie and my cousins and how proud they were and how I was proud for them and how I am proud now for my family. The applauses of approval that we received, I did not believe the accolades were for my service and me alone. But I was more proud for my wife and daughters, they were the ones who truly suffered and sacrificed by my absence for the three years I was gone.

CHAPTER 4

As a youngster, I felt God placed me in a difficult and unique position within this extended family network. I was the oldest within my immediate family. My brother Armand was two years younger than I, and my sister Jacqueline, the baby, four years younger. As close as all our families were, I always felt as if I was somehow misplaced when it came to bonding with my male cousins and fitting in with their youthful experiences. The male cousins on my mother's side were either much older or younger than I. The closest cousins on the Squillante side were my females. On the Cyr side however, there were some cousins who were closer to my age. Uncle Louie had three boys, Billie, Louie and Mike, while Uncle Paul also had a son named Mike. Uncle Pete had a son Emile, who later became a Vietnam vet, who was older, and whom I admired, but again, he was generationally ahead of my age grouping. Because of the logistical living distance between the Cyr clan and us, Rhode Island and Massachusetts, I was not able to grow with them, as I would have liked. Life gets in the way at times. My seeing them as often as possible at Cyr gatherings was not enough to develop the social relationships that bind children in a family, sharing similar experiences which they can relate too in later years. Because of the close living proximity of my mother's family to us, most of my extended family interactions took place on the Squillante side, with Grandpa and Grandma's Water Street residence as the family headquarters. The closest family in sharing both the sociological and environmental situation, as ours, was Aunt Fil and Uncle Johnnie. They lived in the apartment on the first floor of the tenement, in Grandma and Grandpa's house. Teddy, the oldest and only male, was followed by his sister Mary two years older than me and Joannie, one year younger than me. I came to appreciate these cousins as extensions of my family and as brother and sisters. Actually, Teddy, unbeknownst to him and probably to his dismay, became my pseudo-big brother. I'm sure, being the pain I was, he probably didn't want any part of my misadventures or me while I was growing up.

I loved my female cousins, I enjoyed their company, and in fact, I appreciate them more today than ever. But as a young boy, I grew up in a close old-world extended Italian family network. Family, the whole extended family was important, it was the way you identified yourself. There was pride in being identified as a member and belonging. Forever trying to fit in and wanting to belong, to be a part of this extended family group was a way of life. Looking to my male cousins as role models but not able to share and participate in the same experiences as my older cousins, was difficult. Most times in these huge family gatherings, I felt as an outsider. Uncle Londie and his wife, Aunt Alice, had four boys all older than me. They had one daughter, Maria, who was my cousin Joanie's age. Teddy and those cousins, Johnnie, Dickie, Jerry, and Gregory were close and I was too young to fit in, an outsider. Uncle Pat and Aunt Angie had five daughters, the youngest, Angelina, who was my age. Aunt Carrie and Uncle Tony had three girls and one boy. The oldest girl, Karen, was my sister's age. While Uncle Emilio and Aunt Jeanne had two boys and two girls (great family planning), however the oldest, Emilio Junior, was again my sister Jackie's age. Of course, I had friends and classmates my own age, which I socialized and identified, but that wasn't the issue. With a strong immigrant extended family bond, it was an issue of pride of family heritage. All around me it seemed as if each family member was able to band together into a collection of like relatives, age, and sex. They would be able to form groups and be able to relate by age, gender, or like interests, all except me. I seemed to always be the odd man out. I wasn't the right sex, the right age, or sometimes a combination of the two, go figure.

So I had to make myself known, to be accepted, to belong trying to fit in somewhere. As I got older, I realized more and more that this was more of my issue and not of others. I created most of the problems. I was accepted as family but didn't realize this until later in life. Due to the immaturity of my young age, I rationalized that I was to get attention at any cost. My Squillante cousins were always bigger than me and wouldn't hurt me, this I knew. Plus I knew my aunts would always take my side, they always did. I was cute and adorable. My aunts and uncles always attributed my misadventures to being "all boy." I believe they thought of me as the "Dennis the Menace" of the Squillante family. So I was free to start arguments and create issues. I manufactured problems, such as hitting them, daring them to retaliate, challenging them to take notice of me. I tried to excel at sports, to be their equal, and that didn't work either. I was smaller than they were and much less talented. Of course, I didn't realize that all I was doing was making them want to lose me time and time again. Some of the things I did still bring me to smiles and silent laughter, and I can't believe I survived them all.

The female and male cousins always had sleepovers. So naturally, I always wanted to be included and share in the sleepovers also. Well, one of my problems was I sometimes wet the bed. Since Cousin Teddy was the one downstairs in the apartment, he was the one I usually requested to stay overnight. I can remember one night I awoke cold and damp and alone. Teddy had left the bed and sort out the comfort of a dry couch in another room. I knew I couldn't spend the rest of the night in wet clothes and a cold damp bed. So I left the bed in early morning, before anyone woke up, walked through my aunt and uncle's bedroom and to the stairway leading upstairs to our apartment. Our apartment door wasn't locked, went up to the attic, and crawled into bed with my brother Armand. Morning came and Uncle Johnny, Aunt Fil and Teddy couldn't find me in their apartment. They ran upstairs, woke Ma and Dad up, and asked about my whereabouts. Now my parents had no idea where I was either, as everyone was asleep when I went home and everyone naturally became a little concerned. So now it became a treasure hunt to find me. Finally someone checked the attic and found Armand and I sleeping on the mattress on the floor as was our normal pattern. The wetting didn't cause any issue, but the MIA issue was something I had to deal with. No more sleepovers was the order issued for a while. With me, there was always one issue after another. I never really understood what the big deal was when things would happen; hey, no one ever really got hurt much!

The yard on 160 Water Street was no more than a cemented two-car driveway. Grandpa and Grandma's tenement house was L-shaped. Their living room with windows on three walls was on the second floor over the entrance to the basement overlooking the yard. Grandpa would read his paper daily by one of the windows. Well, one day, I decided to hit hard rubber baseballs in the yard. You know, throw the ball up, and take a big swing at it, all the while pretending that you're the hero of the game by belting a homer out of the park in the bottom of the ninth inning. There were really only two problems with that thought. One the yard was too small, and two, Grandpa was sitting by the window. I threw the ball up and took a gigantic swing. The ball crashed through the window that Grandpa was sitting near. But it didn't stop there. It bounced off his head and went through a window on the other side. So that swing resulted in two broken widows and a bump on my grandfather's head. Talk about a hit and bad luck. Times like this, Grandpa would return his vocabulary to his Italian heritage. I really don't know what he said, but it was loud and demonstrative and I was in trouble. Dad had to fix the windows and I wasn't allowed to handle a bat and ball in the yard anymore. So now I had to find something else to do. So I took my interests inside.

I was very close to Grandpa and Grandma in so many ways; their house was my house. As I got older, Grandpa I would partake of his beer and wine on the sidewalk of Water Street. He would bring out his lounge chair and we watch the sun set and he would share his philosophies with me. First he always bought some cheap Italian red wine. It was always good but just cheap. He would take the wine and transfer it into more expensive bottles from other countries. A typical one would be offering someone his "Japanese wine or German wine." It was always the same stuff from Italy, but he always presented it in a more colorful way to guests. I was the gopher, he would say, "Boy, go get the so-and-so wine," and I would go upstairs to his house and have to transfer the wine to whatever bottle he called for. I was continually shaking my head as his guests were praising the wine and saying they should purchase some. Beer was another story. He always offered everyone a beer. When they accepted his request, he gave them a warm room temperature beer. Now I know he had beer in the refrigerator because I use to share it with him. His logic for offering them a warm beer was undeniable however. Again he said, "Boy, if I offered you a beer, how many would you drink and would you take another the next time you visit me?" I told him I wouldn't drink warm beer and not take another later on. His reply, "That's why I give them warm beer, otherwise they drink all mine." So I would have to go to his bedroom and get the beer out of his closet for his guests, all the while knowing Grandpa had beer in the fridge. Later in life, I assisted with some of the nursing care my grandparents required as they attempted to remain in their homes as their lives slowly ended. As the heads of the family and being so close to them, it was difficult seeing them getting older and failing health.

Prior to all these new battery and remote radio-controlled planes and cars, they were controlled by string tethers and powered by small gasoline engines. Usually, and for a normal person, they required a large area outside. Ma and Dad never really learned that they shouldn't give me an opportunity to do something real stupid. They must have had either a lot of faith that I would eventually do the right thing or they blindly loved me. As they say, love is blind and my parents usually paid for their dedication to me. Well, Ma and Dad bought me one of those gas-powered tethered control airplanes. But Ma and Dad really didn't give me all the rules. I wasn't about to take the time to read the directions either, as patience wasn't one of my virtues. In my young age, I definitely needed guidelines and limits. Even if I had guidelines, I probably wouldn't have followed them, but it would have been nice to have them. So I'm in my attic bedroom alone and bored. What the heck might as well see what this plane can do? So I assemble the model, fill the engine with gas, powered it up, and decided to see what it can do in my bedroom. So I clear off my dresser and charge it up. It's making a loud noise, smells terrible as it spurts out smoke and gas and starts to taxi off my dresser. I'm trying to control the flight plan with the tethered strings in a tight flight around the room. Now this model plane takes off and it gains speed in a circle around my room, which I can't control. It starts to bounce off the walls, ceiling and whatever's in the room, finally crashing into the wall. Now there are pieces of plane and gas all over the place. Again, and as usual, this didn't go unnoticed. Ma rushes upstairs and is not amused about what just happen. Again, I'm in trouble and restricted, no more gas-powered planes, ever. Plus I have to clean the room and wait until Dad comes home to hear it from him too.

CHAPTER 5

Cousin Joannie and I were about the same age with me being a year older and her a whole lot smarter. While they were still living on Water Street, Joannie and I would most often play together To this day, we are close cousins and are spouses are friends as well. I feel sorry now and responsible, but I would kind of drag Joannie into some of my idiot schemes. There was the time Joannie and I wanted to replicate the Lone Ranger, a very popular 1950s weekly television show. He was a hero, a masked man, who was on the good side of the law and had silver bullets as his calling card. For those who remember, our change currency was composed mostly of silver in those days. We figured that if we collected enough change, we could melt it on the stove and manufacture our own bullets. So we hoarded and combined our change and stored it until we felt we had enough to melt into bullets. Big problem though, silver change in a pan, on top of an electric stove, does not melt. It doesn't do the pan any good either as the pan started to melt before the coins. And to top it off, we certainly didn't have enough time alone to use the stove without our parents taking notice. So that was another issue I had to deal with; it started to feel like there wasn't anything I could get away with.

The in-laws, my dad, Uncle Johnnie, and Uncle Tony became quite good friends. As the families of the three daughters got together more often, these three outlaws identified and socialized closely with each other. Adult social drinking was a more common theme in those days and didn't quite have the social stigma it does today. So when they got together to relax, it was party time, which was from my memory quite frequent. The common entrance to the basement to our apartment house was by an outside doorway. The stairs where chipped concrete, smaller and narrower than usual and very steep.

The basement floor was dirt, unlevel, and flooded occasionally. You would have to transverse through this dark damp place to pull strings, which switched on small individual light bulbs. Then you would have to reverse the process to return in the dark up the stairs. This was where our kerosene was stored for our apartment furnace until we installed our gas space heater in our apartment. But more important than the storage of our fuel, this is where our dads stored their booze. The beer was sold in racks, not cases. So they would buy racks of beer, which I still occasionally refer to in a liquor store. It became a rite of passage for us cousins to be able to go and get them their booze, mostly the beer, for our dads. It was quite a feat carrying and juggling bottles of beer while navigating the hazards of the basement. We would stuff the bottles in our pockets and wedge them in our waist between our belt lines and tuck the bottles under an arm. The trick was to keep one hand free to pull the strings to shut the lights off in the basement, avoid the support columns in the dark, maintain yourself in the uneven dirt floor, steer clear of the water and stabilize yourself with one hand on the stairway going up the steep stairs to the outside. Not everyone was entrusted with this responsibility; you had to get to a certain age and ability and earn our parents' trust. I can remember waiting for my turn to inherit this honored task. Teddy and the Squillante boys were the first to experience this time-honored tradition. I couldn't wait until the beer baton was transferred to me. Believe it or not, I can remember how proud I felt when it became my turn to go "to the basement" and the responsibility was passed to me. As young as I was, I was pretty resourceful and my dad and uncles gave me plenty of practice time to perfect the art of retrieving the big boys' drinks.

Trying to hang with the big boys always seemed to cause me more issues. I can remember following them into town one day. My cousins kept telling me to go back home, which of course I didn't listen. Well, as we got near the center of Warren, they really didn't want me following them. As I said before, during the fifties and early sixties, the center of Warren was where most of the storefronts were located. It was truly the "center" of town and the older guys would hang mostly at Rod's Grill. Rod's was a New York wiener place.

Wieners, coffee milk, and hanging out were the usual pastime for the boys and girls in those days. I wanted to part of it. I was still a youngster and I shouldn't have been there or going farther and farther away from home. The Protestant Church on the corner Main Street has a wroth iron fence. An interesting fact about this church is that it was the first place that Rhode Island College, later to be named Brown University was first located. Well, my cousins hung me on this fence by the back of my shirt. It took me awhile to wiggle down off the spike, which held up my shirt. By the time, I did free myself they were long gone and I returned home. The first person I told was Aunt Fil, and her son Teddy took a hit for it. My other cousins were involved, but I knew Aunt Fil would later make Teddy do something with me. I'm sure he wasn't too happy about it, but I won by being able to hang with the big boys. How I did it wasn't the point, it was the result that mattered. As I said, my aunts always took my side; I guess they felt bad for my mother or my misadventures caused them to be amused most times.

We always had our meals as a family at five o'clock when Dad came home from work. Usually Ma had some tale to tell Dad of what I did wrong for the day. For some reason, I was uncontrollable at school no matter what grade. In those days, you were sent to the coatroom, stood in the corner, slapped on the knuckles, or tapped on the head with a ruler and one teacher even had me lie under her desk during class. Ma was always called into the classroom to discuss my inability to maintain some sort of decorum in class. Our neighbor, and my fourth grade teacher Miss Rogers, whom I did countless errands for, such as paying bills, shoveling snow, getting her walnut ice cream and groceries, told me she could not place me in an advanced group in the fifth grade because I would cause a distraction to the other students learning. I guess my diagnosis would be some sort of ADHD nowadays, but then I was just a tough kid to handle. So one day Dad comes home at suppertime, oblivious to what happen during the day. Ma's serving a full meal, my brother and sister, Armand and Jackie, are seated at the table crying and I'm not there. Dad takes the bait and asks what's going on and where's Eddy? Ma says she can't take me today and she gave me to the priest. WHAT?

Yep, she couldn't deal with all my issues today and maybe this will somehow straighten me out. She walked me down to our parish priest, Father Maluozo, talked to him awhile and left me there with him. So now, Dad, after a hard day's work, goes to the Italian Church not knowing what he'll find, hoping he hasn't lost me to some "bad boy school." He rings the bell and Father Maluozo invites him in to join us. All we're doing is having dinner and discussing my inability at being a good son. At that point, I was never really worried, I had rationalized that I wasn't going to be there long because I didn't have a suitcase with any of my belongings. I figured I'd get the talking too and then return home. Actually I didn't get in much trouble that day because Ma and Dad had words about Ma abandoning me, or donating me, or whatever without discussing it with him first. Dad never really said that Ma shouldn't have done it, just not without some family time discussion first. Hearing my parents' discussions sort of oddly hit me. They weren't arguing about sending me to the priest, they were deciding how to discuss it before they sent back to him at a later date! After that incident, I felt I might be making more trips to the priest, but it never happened again.

During this time, about the second or third grade, I developed an interesting physical ailment. I was allergic to insect bites. Not just to the normal type allergy of bees or wasps' stings, but to mosquitoes and just about any insect bites. I would swell and become lethargic and sweaty, sometimes developing breathing issues. Initially Ma would bring me to Uncle Londie's and he would treat me with oral or injectable meds and I would sleep for hours. The situation was getting more prevalent and acute. So Uncle Londie sent me to an allergist, Dr. Friedman in Providence. After the initial testing I was found to be allergic to quite a number of insects, this was when I was in the third grade. I would have to go during the summer every four weeks for desensitization injections. During the winter, I was given the luxury of going to seven or eight weeks before I needed the injections. The teachers didn't want to have any responsibility for my health care during this time and wanted me at the first indication of any reaction to be released home. Because they had extra cars, whenever I was bitten during the school year, my Aunts Carrie and

Jeanne would always be called to school to take me home. Initially, I was quite sick when I would be bitten. At home, Ma would nurse me, spoil me, give me meds, and off to sleep I would go. Very early I found this to be an advantage. So naturally, I began to use this to my own self-interest. I found that I could seek out certain insects, which would bite me, not make me really sick and I could be released form school at my convenience. This was my routine until I entered my first year at Providence College in 1969. As you know the Vietnam War was at its peak in 1969. The draft lottery was just initiated. I felt that I was secure and safe in possession of this lethal allergic allergy, not being draftable into the army. This was my ticket out! After all, Vietnam and its lush green and bug-infested country would be a terrible place with such a lethal insect allergy. So I go to the doc's office with the proper paperwork for a deferment. After about ten years of therapy, I figured this doctor would easily document my inability to serve, especially in Vietnam. The doc when presented with the paperwork said, "I'm not signing that, you can serve." What! I went here for ten years, continually getting these stupid injections. My parents not buying a real Christmas tree for fear of insects and having to burden my family with the stigma of a pink artificial Christmas tree year after year. To this day, I'm held as the sole reason for this embarrassing childhood memory. I pleaded my case but the doc said I was okay, I was cured and I should serve. Well, I took the last injection, paid the fee, and never went back. Ma and Dad wanted me to return to actually get the completed bill of health from him, as a final closure. I told them if I get drafted, I'd send him my welcome notice from the government to the US Army. My allergy ended in that instant.

CHAPTER 6

As a youngster, I always seemed to be able to complete my school work just enough to pass, sometimes just barely. Things just always seemed to be a little different for me. In English, I read the wrong words, spelled them wrong, and was not able to see the word in my mind or sound them out phonically to spell them. In math, the numbers were jumbled or placed frequently in the wrong order. I can remember how confused I felt at times. However, I never felt I wasn't intelligent enough. I knew I wasn't the brightest bulb on the Christmas tree, but I truly knew I had the intelligence to compete with my classmates. My thought process was right, but the answers were wrong because of the sequencing issues. Studying was never that easy and because the words didn't flow and sometimes not recognized, the meaning of the reading would be lost. English and math almost cost me my future lifestyle. Learning was becoming more of a hardship as I went through each class. It was difficult for me to share this problem with others. No one else seemed to have this issue and no one ever talked about this particular problem. I didn't know how to explain this to anyone at times, I didn't see what they were seeing or I saw it differently. The summer after the fifth grade I had to go to summer school for both math and English. I had done so terribly in grade five that year in both subjects. I had given up in that fifth year. It was too hard to try to figure out the reason I wasn't on the same page as my classmates. In order to be promoted to the next grade, the pressure was on; I would have to pass both math and English in summer school. I knew I had to do something. I had to devise a method that would slow me down and concentrate on each letter or numeral. The method that seemed to work best for me was to copy and write and rewrite everything over and over again. It was a slow process, to replicate the work in my own hand. Yet I was able to see and concentrate on what I was placing on the paper and compare it to the assigned work and note the differences. It caused me to focus and to continually reassess. I started with numbers, and somehow it worked in math, so I took this method to my English class. I began to rewrite and copy the assigned work, then complete the assignment. I started to have success and I did well that summer. From that point on, school made a little more sense and I wasn't the odd person out in class anymore. This is the study method I still do to this day. I write it out, rewrite it, and then write it again and again, over and over. Today, I still cannot see the spelling of a word in my brain; I can't correctly spell a word phonically. I use my wife, kids, and spell check. Numbers are still jumbled, but I repeat and review and re-read, never allowing myself to feel comfortable with just a once over review. I am constantly rechecking my work. After this enlightenment, I was beginning to feel successful, to be almost normal. I began to believe in myself and that I could actually compete with others. The greatest issue I still have to this day, which has affected some of my life-decisions is that of learning a foreign language. I have great difficulty trying to take some foreign word and processing it cerebrally and then attempting to correctly pronounce it. The letters, words, and sounds don't connect for me. This difficulty has followed me throughout my life as I failed French II in high school and had to repeat it in order to qualify for college. Then in my first year of college, I barely passed Spanish and because of this a career path was later altered. Later in life, I was actually accepted to medical school in Guadalajara, Mexico, but declined the acceptance because I knew I would not be able to compete in a foreign language.

With this new gained scholastic revolution however, I hit my stride. I was experiencing a newfound success. As I entered the sixth grade I was scholastically a better student. From that point on, school wasn't the burden it had always been. School still wasn't easy, it required extra work to be somewhat successful, but I could see a sunrise rather than a sunset in my future. These new confidences in me lead to my being more socially outgoing and accepted. My relationships with friends and family became more stabilized. Feeling more confident and solid in myself, I started to seek more outside interests. I focused upon the sport of basketball. Basketball started to become a major focus in my life. Basketball was a method to socialize with peers my own age. More importantly, it was away I could compete with my cousins, even though I was always chosen last. Always smaller, I became a dribbler and a playmaker. Once I had the ball, I owned the game; they had to wait until I surrendered the ball. So more often than not, I usually held the ball far too long, and this caused great contestation to my cousins. Basketball is also a sport of isolation; all you need is a ball, a hoop, an imagination and hours to dream while practicing skills. The loneliness of the sport also gave me the opportunity to fantasize while attempting to bridge the age gap within the family hierarchy. I could spend hours upon hours dribbling, shooting, and passing alone, trying to gain the skills to impress the older cousins and become their equal. Basketball could be my equalizer with my cousins and I partially believed I was somewhat successful. To this day, I still receive the comments about my dribbling and in never wanting to relinquish the ball. We laugh about it now, but it served me well as I accomplished what I had set out to do, compete with and against them on their level.

As a freshman, I entered Warren High School in 1965. Warren High was a small school having four classes, freshman through senior years, with a total of maybe six hundred students' tops. You could easily have a conversation with each student in the school and know them by name by the end of the school year. My cousin Mary, Aunt Fil's oldest daughter, was a senior. Mary was popular and confident. She also was my benefactor. She made it a personnel quest to tell the teacher's and her fellow seniors that I was her cousin and not to give me a difficult time. I appreciated this thoughtfulness and reciprocated this act by paving the way in the same manner for my brother and cousins as they entered high school. I don't know if it had the same effect as Mary had on my entrance into high school, but I tried. High school was a landmark turning point in my life; it was the door to adulthood. The conduit was through high school, but the path to adulthood was longer and more distorted than I could ever realize. Adulthood looked so easy and clear back then. Moving toward adulthood through high school is an arrogant overconfident affair. Missing is the adult experience of life with its pains, wounds, hardships, and true selfless sacrifices. High school offers an illusion, a taste of adulthood within a protected bubble shielding each student from most of socialites' responsibilities. Consequences for this experimentation into quasi-adults decisions are most often tapered and second chances are expected and given. I found high school was the learning platform to maturity through a progress from selfishness to magnanimous, from cause to effect and from irresponsibleness to accountability. At the end of the year, Mary presented my mother and me with extra admission tickets into her senior class's graduation exercise. I still can visualize my cousin in one of the back rows, dressed in the white gown, mortarboard on her head, and the maroon and white tassel off to the side. She spotted me in the audience, and throughout the ceremony, she flashed me numerous smiles and thumbs-up signs. I often wonder why, with so many other cousins, especially female, Mary chose me as an extra to attend her graduation. Maybe she knew that I needed the validation for the next three years ahead of me. That the impact of my being present at her graduation ceremony, witnessing the successful completion of high school and the awarding of a diploma was the energy I needed to see my own high school career to completion. Maybe not, maybe that's placing a more existential meaning to a simple act of kindness. But maybe, just maybe, it was planned by Mary to show me, a troubled and sometimes difficult cousin, the way to success and a joyful closure to a high school career. For whatever the reason, she chose well. Attendance at her graduation actually did make a huge impact upon me. Now I not only wanted to finish high school, get a degree, and leave, but I now wanted to enjoy the experience of high school to its fullest. I had witnessed the joy of the high school experience. Mary had demonstrated this past year with her passion and involvement in both the academic and social aspects of how high school can be both. She had been a role model for my freshman year, and now as she graduated, she was leaving me a path for a successful high school future.

In my remaining high school years, friends took on more of an influential role. They began to offset the closeness of my cousins and family. With these associations, I began paving my way in to adulthood. Basketball was now becoming a major owner of my time. Basketball not only gave me enjoyment from playing the sport, but also more importantly was the intermediary to both male and now newfound relationships with "girls." It was a way to relate to both genders. I earned a spot on the freshman, junior varsity, and varsity teams up through to my junior year. Basketball kept me busy year round; during the summer, I was involved in basketball leagues in the neighboring town of Bristol and Warren and attended a summer basketball camp held by the two coaches form local colleges and universities. My junior year everything changed with basketball. It wasn't as rewarding, in fact it caused me my greatest disappointment in high school. My junior year I earned a spot on the varsity team. Normally, twelve students were on the team. This year, the coach only carried ten members. I did start a number of games and played in a few after I lost my starting position. The coach never approached me and explained why or for what reason my playing time was lessened. As an adult, I can rationalize now that I held some of responsibility to seek out the reason for my benching. But I wasn't the adult; the coach was the adult leader. As the coach, it was his job to actually coach, teach, tutor, prepare, instruct, and console. There was none of this. Even now, after all these years, I still harbor hurt and discontent on how he managed me as a young player. I still to this day do not have an understanding as to why he made the decisions he made. It wasn't and never was the decision to not play me. But it was his lack of explaining the reason he chose not to play me and why his abandonment of his coaching me, that hurt.

As I said, there were ten members of our team. After the season, around February, an assembly was held in the school auditorium with the entire high school body in attendance to distribute awards to the players for the winter sport season. At Christmas, Ma and Dad gave me a white letter sweater, as our school colors were maroon and white, in the anticipation of my earning a varsity maroon letter "W." It would have been my highlight of my high school sport's career. An outward statement of my success, an accomplishment, something I earned and would wear during school designating me as an elite athletic member. Now I understand how shallow that thought process was. But I had worked long hours, sacrificed, and dedicated myself for that simple letter "W." We were supposed to be individually acknowledged by the coach and presented with our certificates and letters on stage. The coach awarded only eight of the highly valued letters with certificates. Just two of us received only certificates, the last two announced. When my time arrived, he presented me with only a certificate, a piece of paper that really only stated I was a member of the team. My mind was busy, disappointment, anger as he held out that sole piece of paper. As a family, financially, we didn't have much. I knew how much the sweater cost, that Ma and Dad gave me, and the sacrifice they made to purchase one for me. How proud they were when I opened their gift on Christmas day for them anticipating and expecting me to be awarded the letter. How was I to face them at home with only this certificate? In front of the school, I took the certificate, crumbled it, and attempted to return to my place on stage. The coach called me back and said, "Eddy, my hand." I did a quick about face presented my hand, never closed it to encompass his, and walked away. I was crushed, but more importantly, I was hurt for my parents. How was I to tell them that I failed and their gift would not be used? The coach never talked to me after, never asked me why, never sort a closure to this issue. Mr. Tsommes, the assistant principal, later talked with me in private to discuss why I made an issue at the assembly. Later he actually gave me the high school athletic letter, but I would never wear it. How could I? The school had witnessed my rebellion. But it was too late by then, by the time he presented me with the letter, on my own, I had dyed the sweater gold. My parents had made a sacrifice in purchasing the sweater, denying themselves and maybe my brother and sister of a Christmas gift. My parents never required me to wear the sweater, but I wanted to wear it for them, I had to wear it for them. I understood their love in sacrificing of them for me. I wore the gold sweater the remaining time through high school. Never placing the letter on the sweater. I still have that sweater and the letter separately stored away. The coach left for California after my junior year. But I didn't try out for basketball my senior year.

Basketball was over, I moved on to another endeavor, something I was more successful and appreciated.

Prior to the end of my junior year, the drama coach, Mr. Marcello, approached me and asked me to audition for the spring show. A little unsure at this new endeavor he was proposing, I asked him what play and role he had in mind for me. He explained that he was going to present "You're a Good Man Charlie Brown," and he thought I would be able to secure the part of Snoopy. Well, from that point on, my high school experience began to be more promising and enjoyable. Mr. Marcello had taken me as a troubled outcast and given me a chance to excel and demonstrate to both classmates and educators that I indeed had some value and talent. I became more confident in my abilities and myself. I never imagined the accomplished success I would enjoy as a member of the drama club. The roles I was blessed with my senior year were not only Snoopy, but also the king in "The King and I" and George M. Cohen in our senior minstrel. With the increasing success of these roles, it became easier for me to interrelate with my classmates at their level and no longer harbor such feelings of not being an equal to my peers in sports. Not only did the school environment acknowledge my success, but the community as well commented upon my acting ability. This was all new to me; I had never before had the recognition for success as I now enjoyed. On senior night, I was awarded the most talented male senior in theater arts. It was the first time I was the "Most" in anything. The success of my drama accomplishments began to spill over to other endeavors within my life.

I'm learning that hard work in one thing can lead to an advantage in another. After the production of "You're a Good Man Charlie Brown," my next-door neighbor, Mr. Vitullo, a member of the Warren Town Council approached me with a proposition. Warren was covered by the state senatorial district of Bristol, our larger neighboring town. State Senator Bruno wanted to secure a more popular vote by appointing someone from the north end of Warren as his Page in the State Senate. Mr. Vitullo, after seeing me as Snoopy, suggested me as his candidate. Senator Bruno selected me as a senior in high school. I was to be a Rhode Island State Senate Page two days per week. I held this position for a total of six years. This included my senior year in high school along with my five college years representing both the Democrat and Republican parties at the state house. There was a clinch however prior to accepting this position. I had to acquire permission to leave school as an early dismissal for the two required days in the senate. In my senior year, I was in a third division English class, which out of six divisions was right in the middle of academic aptitude. My third division English was the last class of the day and a requirement for graduation, which I was not allowed to miss. The teacher, Mrs. Parks was the instructor for both the third and first division English classes. I would have to get her permission to switch from the third to first division, which was at an earlier time in the daily class schedule. I can remember her warning, that the first division was a high functioning class, and she would not tolerate any less than my operating at my highest potential. I told her I really wanted this position as senate page and I would not fail her. I didn't fail her, and at year-end, I was a "B" student and a competitive classmate in this advanced English class. Mrs. Parks later told me that she had confidence in my abilities and me, but she knew I needed some type of catalyst to ignite my potential. I found Mrs. Parks as an educator who had faith in me and demanded me to challenge my potential, and she gave me an opportunity to prove myself.

Senior year I had a fire engine red 1962 Chevy II car, which was involved in an accident and was repaired prior to my purchasing it. Mechanically, it ran pretty good, except when it rained. The rainwater would somehow get into the car and collect on the floorboards, forming mini-lakes. I would have to vacuum and sponge the water out. My solution to this problem was to drill holes in the floorboards to allow the water to drain out. A major drawback to that solution was the fumes from the exhaust would be drawn into the car as well as the cold weather. To solve these issues, I had to ride with the windows partly open and the heater on full blast in the winter. During this time in my senior year, I would drive to the Rhode Island State Senate as a Senate Page. Continuing with my haphazard luck, my first day as a senate page while driving the Chevy II to the state house in January 1969, I got a flat tire. With a jacket, tie, and white shirt,

I changed the tire by the side of the road. I showed up as the only high school page that year to the state house, covered in mud and grease. The Head Page of the Senate immediately sent me home. I made a better appearance the next time as I made it without incident. I never considered the page position as a job. It was always an experience, which I was always felt grateful and fortunate to possess, one that many others would not be able to experience. I was witnessing politics, policies, and the process of government from inside Rhode Island. And I was able to use that process for an incident, which was able to get me out of a predicament at high school.

As a senior in the last semester, there were times that I thought I was above the rules. So early spring, with the weather warming, I decided to take a day off, with my friends and enjoy freedom from the education process. Well, we got caught and we had to face the assistant principal, Mr. Tsommes. Our payment for the truancy was after school detention for two weeks. The senate was in full swing and I didn't want to jeopardize my position as a page. So I explained to Mr. Tsommes that the entire State of Rhode Island and Providence Plantations needed my expertise to effectively function correctly. Of course, he didn't buy it, but he offered me a challenge, which he believed I wouldn't be able to meet. He said if I could get a note validating my need to be at the state house he would forgo my detention time. It has changed now, but during this time, the Lieutenant Governor was the President Pro Temp of the Senate. Lt. Governor Garrahy daily presided over the Senate, and although he didn't personally know me, recognized me as a permanent member of the senate pages. I approached him with my dilemma. I was painfully honest with him. Explaining that I took the day off from school illegally was caught and now I have to serve my time in detention for two weeks rather than come to the senate. I offered him a plea. If he would write a letter, explaining to the assistant principal that I was needed here in the senate, signed by him, the Lt. Governor, I could be excused from detention and could continue with my page obligations. The Lt. Governor looked at me and laughed, said he would do it, just this once, but I had to promise never to repeat this action again. Of course I said I would, and I never did. Laughing to myself, all I could imagine was bringing in a letter from the Lt. Governor explaining how important I was to the State of Rhode Island.

Well, by the end of the senate session that day, I was called up to the Lt. Governor's office and presented with the official letterhead and signature of Lt. Governor Joseph Garrahy. The letter explained that I was invaluable to the normal functioning of the State of Rhode Island and would the assistant principal Mr. Tsommes please excuse me from detention. Truthfully I didn't believe I could pull this off, but I did. The next morning arriving at school I headed straight to the assistant principal's office. I had an overconfident smugness and presented him with the official announcement of my importance to the State. He took the letter sheepishly and became to read it in disbelieve. He just began to laugh loudly and questioned if it was real. After much personnel examination and in conference with some other administrators and educators, they all decided it was in fact the real deal. Mr. Tsommes kept both his word and the letter. He said I was excused from detention this time, but this excuse would only work once. If I was to screw up again, not even a letter from the President of the United States would get me out of detention next time. I learned years later after I left high school that Mr. Tsommes later died of cancer. A true tragedy, he was tough, always fair, and able to relate with most students and command their respect. He understood my issue with the basketball coach, never judged me wrongly, and reinforced and supported my positive attributes.

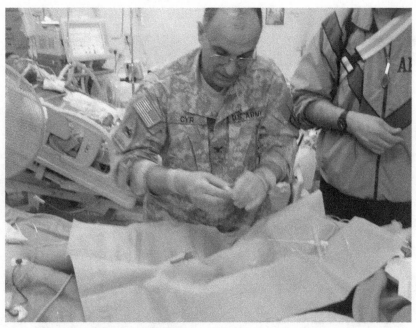

COL Cyr placing nerve blocks to reduce pain
and preparing patient for air evacuation

Daughter, CPT.
Rachelle Cyr

Father of COL Cyr"s family
military history

Daughter, MAJ.
Jessica Stanley

LTC Cortella and COL Cyr Guard Duty Christmas day

Christmas Day

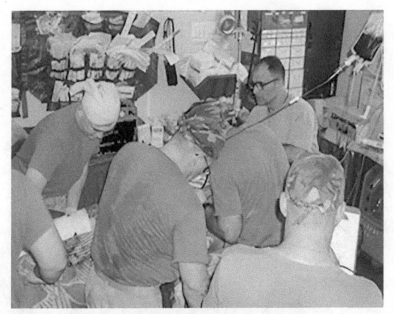

2003 COL Cyr and the Forward Surgical
Team treating multi-trauma

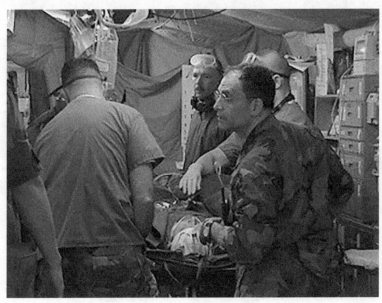

2001 COL Cyr and the 399th Combat Support
hospital team in the Emergency area

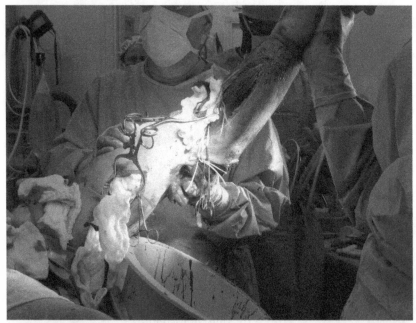

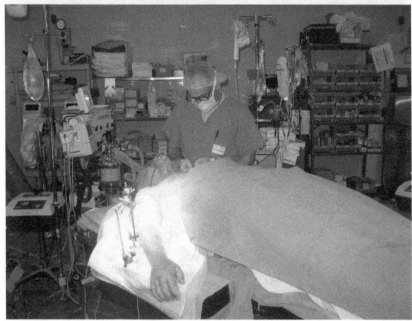

Multi-trauma patients

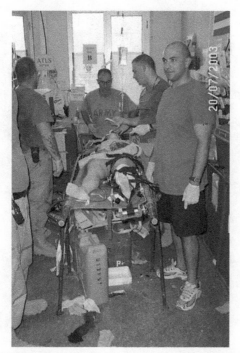

The 912th FST team treating a multi-trauma
patient and preparing for air evacuation

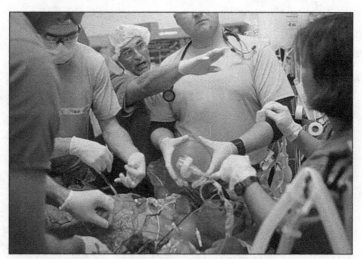

Permission by Boston Globe given Colonel Edward O. Cyr, chief
of anesthesia, issued instructions as a 399th surgical team fought
to save a severely wounded man. (Dominic Chavez/ Globe Staff)

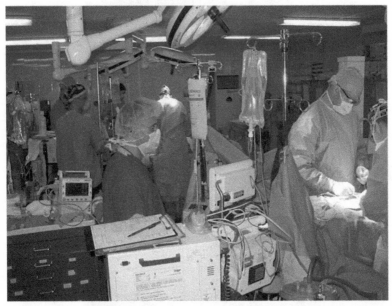

The operating room at Mosul

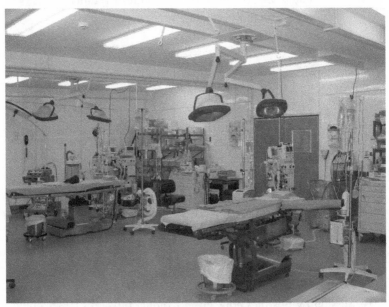

The operating room at AlAsad

Patricia Cyr, Father Masello (our Parish Priest), COL Eddie Cyr

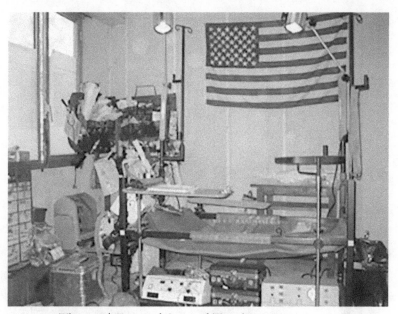

The 912th Forward Surgical Team's operating room

Top Row: Renee, Jessica, Rachelle
Bottom Row; Kary-Anne, Patricia, Jennifeer

COL Cyr on Convoy to other FST's for supplies

COL Cyr at Saint Mother Theresa's Church
during the Kosovo deployment

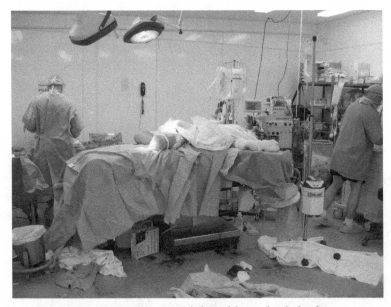

Common trauma with horrible multiple limb
loss, seen frequently at our hospitals

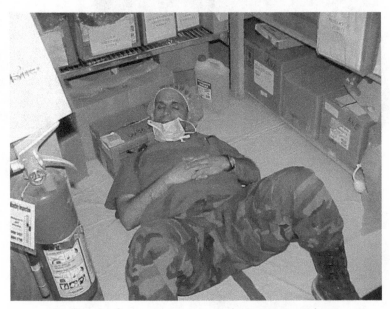

Grabbing a few quick snoozes in between procedures,
after administering anesthesia all night

CHAPTER 7

From freshman year in high school and for about fifteen continuous years, I held various jobs within the Wharf Tavern restaurant in Warren, near my house on Water Street. Uncle Emilio was the person who helped secure this position for me. As a fifteen-year-old high school freshman at the "Wharf," my first position was "pot man." This required you to be in a little room with three large sinks and wash every pot used in the restaurant. It was the worst job in the place. When you arrived at work at around five PM, there was already a mountain of pots and pans that the cooks had used to begin their prep work. Once the customers arrived, there was a never-ending march of dirty pots and pans to clean. The "pot man" was the very last person to finish the night, even behind the dishwashers. The wharf was located on the waterfront with docks on three sides. The pot room had a small window, which overlooked a small inlet where the owner of the Wharf docked his forty-one foot yacht. As a young and new employee, that was my position, pot man. So one of my fist days on the job, with what I felt as an insurmountable number of pans and pans to clean, I devised a plot to rid me of this nemesis. So I decided to throw the most soiled pots and pans out the window in the river. Then I began to discard the less soiled ones. Then the impulse was stronger than I. I couldn't control myself; I began throwing out more and more pots and pans. They would hit the water, skim the top of the river, then slowly and almost musically and rhythmically, swing to and fro while sinking to the bottom. That night, I remember the cooks marveled that as a new employee, I was always ahead of the rush of dirty pans to clean. I also finished the evening earlier than any of my counterparts previously.

Upon my arrival to work the next day, I was told to report to the owners of the restaurant immediately. The owner of the Wharf Tavern's house was in front of the inlet in which their yacht was docked. It appeared that all evening, I had discarded the pots and pans at high tide. The problem with high tide is that low tide follows. At low tide, washed ashore was an array of dirty pots and pans. The owners couldn't miss the obvious as the shore was covered with bright aluminum and steeled pots and pans practically right in front of their doorway. Once the owners had asked the cooks what happen and who was in the pot room, I was doomed. So I marched up to their house expecting to be fired in my first week on the job. He asked me to truthfully tell him what happened and why I threw the pots and pans out. I told him they were dirty and there were too many and I couldn't keep up the pace. He laughed, told me that was why I was there, and what should he do with me. I replied that I thought he was going to fire me. I just stood there waiting for his decision. He told me he would give me another chance. But I had to go to the shore at low tide, retrieve all the pots and pans, wash them and "pots" was my permanent position for the time being. So that's what I did. Throughout my career at the Wharf, I held a variety of positions, to include, dishwasher, short order cook, waiter, maître'd, and cleaning crewmember. During my fifteen years there, I met many wonderful honest, hardworking people. Three of my favorites were Dolores and Tweet (Ed) Zeberswki and Al Daunghlt. Tweet was a World War II enlisted infantryman, who had fought in Europe. They were a continuous thread throughout my development from my teenage years to early adulthood until I left the Wharf at about the age of thirty-three.

High school was a complicated but an enjoyable episode of my life. It was where I began to understand the complexities of friendships and relationships. Most of these associations have been lifelong friends and acquaintances. Together, as a class, we shared in the growth of each of us from childhood to early adulthood. As we have matured into our adult patterns, the innocence of our high school relationships have helped to define the path we took into adulthood. Now at our present ages, there is no longer any a comparison or judgments between us. We are accepted as equals now; time has taken away the competiveness and we wish each other only the best of health and happiness. High school was where I learned that I could be a friend equally with each gender. Coming from such an ethnic family background, this was earth shattering for me. Previously, I thought the purpose of the opposite gender was to respect them, find a mate, settle down, and raise a family. During these high school years, I genuinely came to appreciate women as true friends, peers, confidants, and most times superior to males. It was a good thing I recognized this early in my adulthood. Later in life, as the father of five daughters and being a nurse in a predominately female profession, I was forever reminded and accepting of the female superiority. Life is full of ironies. My first dating experience and steady girlfriend was as a senior in high school. Gloria was very pretty, talented, and tolerable of my intellectual shortcomings. She was also was the class valedictorian of our 1969 high school class, a world-class musician, and was accepted to the Ivy League school, Brown University. We have remained friends, and in fact, Gloria retired as a lieutenant colonel from the US Air Force.

Meanwhile, in my senior year, I was having difficulty gaining admission to a four-year college. As mentioned previously, I had difficulty with math and English. This became more evident as I approached graduation with decisions for my future. I took the College Board entrance exams a number of times and barely scored over five hundred in either of them, only once. The achievement tests the results were even worse, my first time taking the English achievement I scored an earth-shattering two hundred and eighty and math was in the high three hundreds. The issue with those scores is that in both the college boards and achievement tests they gave you two hundred points for just writing your name. This caused great anguish in my household. My guidance director's suggestion was for me to save any money for college, join the military, and buy a nice car. My mother was beside herself and I can remember our meetings with the guidance director mapping out enrolling in a preparatory school prior to a junior college. Funny though, I never felt that I wasn't going to college, that somehow I would get accepted somewhere.

So, I kept taking the exams until the scores were at least somewhat reasonable for applications. These tests always frightened me. I had no way to prepare for them, most times we couldn't write in the booklets, and the time limit made it difficult for me to rewrite or review the questions over so that I could get the sequencing correct. But I did get accepted to a number of schools, one being Providence College, which at the time was my first choice.

I had saved most of my money throughout high school in anticipation of my going to college. As a commuter, the tuition at Providence College that first year was thirty-three hundred dollars ($3,300). My parents helped me all that they could and sacrificed for my brother, sister's higher education, and mine. However, the financial responsibility at the private college was really more than I could afford. I was forced to work three different jobs while attending school to afford the tuition. I initially had ambitions on going to medical school. But the academic course work was intense that first year and coupled with my work requirement didn't allow me to concentrate on my studies. The required academics were biology, chemistry, foreign language (Spanish), calculus (which I never had in high school), and English composition. I just found it impossible to maintain the grades, work so many hours, and commute to college. At the end of my first year at Providence College, I came to a stark realization that it was futile to continue to matriculate there with my average so low and not enough resources to finance the rest of my college career. And if I decided not to attend college, for even a semester, there was one other another issue to deal with—the draft!

The summer following this first year of college was monumental and life-changing for all males within this same year group. In 1970–71, the draft lottery was in effect and the Vietnam War was at its peak. Interestingly, in late spring, I attended an anti-war rally at Providence College with a high school friend, Jodie, who incidentally ended up marrying my cousin Joannie. The interesting part was that this rally had Catholic priests as partial organizers and principle speakers. We later walked down from the college en masse and blocked an intersection on Smith Street. We stayed there for a while, made a lot of noise, no real issue arose, and we all later were dismissed without any real incident. The shooting of the students at a rally at Kent State happened and escalated the anti-war sentiment on the college campuses. As the anti-war movement began to gain momentum, fear took over the college scene and the colleges feared that more fatal incidents would occur. So to quell the surge of demonstrations on campuses the colleges and university canceled most of the final exams across the nation. Thus, the schools ended the academic year early to defuse any more lethal incidents on college campuses nationwide, in hope that the students would just return home. I learned of my draft number, I believe in 1971 on the ride home with my dad from Mountop Electric Company, where I had summer employment. Listening to the radio, I knew that my future and maybe my life were dependent on dumb blind luck. There were three people I knew personally from my hometown, who had gone to Vietnam and were killed. A person from our church, one of my cousin Mary's high school classmates and one of my classmates who left school early in our senior year to join the military. My ear was glued to the radio as they were reading the results of the lottery. Then the date of my birthday, January 13, was announced, pause, my breath was held, I stopped breathing, a thousand thoughts raced through my head, then I heard it, three hundred and thirty (330)! Only one friend ended up with a low number. Paul had the number two overall in the draft. However, he was classified as not being draftable due to his multiple knee injuries and surgeries, so he was safe also. We made it as a group, all our numbers where high enough, in avoiding the draft; we were relieved and thankful, celebrating with a night of drinking beer at Brown Street in Warren. Celebrating at Brown Street, normally our common area for "parking" with our girls. This was the ultimate boys' night out. In our celebration and gratitude to the gods. We did salute those who were not as fortunate as we were, especially those who had made the sacrifice and would not come home.

Prior to the end of the spring semester at Providence College, I began to look at both the Rhode Island State College and University as an affordable avenue to my career goals. I was accepted into the biology secondary education program at Rhode Island College (RIC).

The tuition was far more reasonable and affordable at one hundred and twenty-five dollars ($125) per semester. One of the requirements for acceptance into the college was for me to retake the initial biology two-semester courses over at RIC, unless I could pass the equivalency exam. I passed the exam quite easily and was able to enroll into an advanced biology curriculum. I did quite well that first year being able to concentrate more on my studies, as the finances were not as much an issue.

At the time, Rhode Island College was beginning a nursing program. Doing some research about the program, I found out I would be in the initial graduating class. But I would have to be a college student for a total of five years, including the year I spent at Providence College, rather the four-year tract I was now enrolled. Being an education major during this time frame, 1970s, was a very difficult. Teaching jobs in the Rhode Island areas were extremely difficult to acquire. My priorities began to change, getting older I began to lose the innocence of life without financial stability. Personally, I felt there was no way I could spend four years in college, graduate, and not have a teaching job guarantee. The realities of adult life began to loom larger and began to forge my decision-making ability. I never regretted my life on Water Street. The memories of my childhood there are forever embedded in a place that was secure and surrounded by a loving, supported family. But my parents suffered because of lack of plain old money. In comparison to where I wanted to go in my adulthood, what I wanted to accomplish, and that I wanted more financial security, I had to extend my horizons and goals beyond Water Street; I had decisions and concessions to make. All my other relatives had successfully moved away, secured for themselves and their families a more financial and social independence in other geographical areas. Why couldn't I do the same? I had to self-exam what my needs would be to succeed and I would have to redefine what goals I would strive for. I had seen what good my Uncle Lonnie had accomplished as a health provider and how revered he was to those he had helped. Health care was the profession of the future; I would never be without a job. How could I lose? As a nurse, I might never be rich, but I could help people and never worry about my future families' financial success or mine. So nursing was to become my default choice.

So I made the required course change at the college from secondary education to the College of Nursing. That night at the dinner table, I made the announcement to Ma and Dad. Dad just looked at Ma and said, "Where did we go wrong?" Then he asked me "if I was a little funny," meaning sexual preferences. I couldn't help laughing, as did Jackie and Armand, Ma had the look on her face of there goes Eddy again, doing something stupid. I tried to explain to both parents my reasons for the curriculum change. Ma appeared to agree readily with my thoughts. But Dad was a product of the Depression. He believed in the concept of loyalty and stability of being employed lifelong by the same employer and changing careers was not a good decision. Besides, this nursing idea was new and was predominantly a female occupation. Men didn't really go into nursing, not real men, anyway at this time. Throughout my career changes, Dad was always questioning my reason for change. He never really fully appreciated the need to challenge and change the stability of each position I was currently engaged. But things were changing in the '70s. As youngsters, we were not inclined to believe in the omnipotence of the establishment and trust someone else with our futures. Trusting our futures to either big business or government was not how we wanted to invest ourselves. We wanted to be the decision makers of our destiny, and that was how I felt. It was my future and I wanted to decide on my career, this was my choice. Dad eventually agreed with my decision, in fact it was the very next day. How did he see my position so quickly? He went to work and explained that his oldest son wanted to be a nurse and what did they think. When these male maintenance, cleaners, and generator operators at the electric company all thought this was a good career decision, then Dad acquiesced. That night at the dinner table, Dad gave me his blessing that he thought this was a good idea and career move for me.

Entering Rhode Island College of Nursing was truly the choice, which formed the foundation for the rest of my life. I was the first of the Cyrs to enter college, which I knew made my dad proud. The decision to enter and complete the Bachelor of Nursing degree, without my knowledge at the time, was the stepping-stone to my future successes in career, family life and happiness. I was one of 6–8 males in a class of approximately 70 females and 2 of the male students were married! So initially from my viewpoint, there were many more advantages to this new career choice than just the education! There was one issue with that thought process though, I started dating one particular fellow student and never dated another. Initially, I approached this lovely little girl, a year younger than me, about dating her friend. Her friend's response was she thought I was cute! Me cute! Come on now! No one ever said I was cute! It's a nice way to say, "You gotta be kidding me, and I'm not interested in him, and probably never will." Honestly though, she was dating someone else and getting serious. So that option was closed. Yet navigating through this relationship triangle, I developed a certain fondness for this lovely little girl. I approached and asked this lovely little girl out on a first date. Patricia Croy was someone special. Truly special and has been special for 44 years. I still joke with her that she put something in my salad, and I had no choice but to fall in love with her.

During this time, I had long hair, a handlebar mustache, and always wore the military field jacket. By wearing that military jacket seemed normal, a part of my personality, making a statement for my relatives who served and sacrificed. My first date with Patricia ironically was on Memorial Day to see the *Fiddler on the Roof*, with Tevye and the issues of his 5 daughters. What was ironic, later as mentioned I served over 30 years in the military, so Memorial Day is something special for anyone with a service connection. Memorial Day is a time to remember all those who sacrificed in uniform. But truly ironic is that Patricia and I were fortunate to be blessed with 5 daughters. Fortunate may not be the best word to describe, but blessed is, as I believe I have earned my place through those Golden Gates raising 5 daughters. Meeting Tricia's family that first time was a unique experience. But it was that experience of Tricia's familial background, which instantly drew us closer. Tricia is the middle child with 10 siblings, with a strong Catholic faith. Her older sisters had serious boyfriends, and her parents at the time had taken in foster children. So that first date meeting was quite an initiation into the Croy family mob. But because of my extended family relationships, this seemed normal and comfortable to me. Tricia's family also had a background of service to our country. Her father, Stanley, was a Word War II and Korean War veteran, he was a Pharmacist Mate in the Navy. Tricia's older sister, Janet's husband Paul, was in the Rhode Island National Guard. Tricia's older brother, Butch, had served three years in the army stationed in Germany, and in the near future, two of her younger brothers also joined the military, Danny also enlisted in the Rhode Island National Guard and Kevin joined the Air Force Reserves. In every direction I took, those close to me demonstrated military service. It was as if my career path was leading me to putting a uniform on.

During my student-nursing career, in 1973, two things occurred early that I can still remember so vividly, and each time it brings me laughable moments at my inexperience at that time in my career. The first occurred with my initial patient assignment at Rhode Island Hospital as a student. The patient was a ninety-year-old gentleman recovering from a cardiac condition. So I get my assignment, studied his medical condition, the meds he needed, the nursing assessments, signs and symptoms of any substantial issues. So I'm confident, bold, knowledgeable and head down to his room. What I find is this old man sitting up in his bed, eyes closed, mouth open, not responding to my calling his name. Now I'm panicking, I start to call for help, call a code, stat CPR. All hell is breaking loose; people are rushing in, medical students, interns, residents, and nurses, my instructor! Well, it appears the patient wakes up from a peaceful sleep, his hearing aid was turned off, because there was too much noise for him to rest. Ah, yeah, so that was my first crisis, I began thinking maybe nursing wasn't my best choice.

Another screw-up occurred as a position of orderly at the Union Hospital in Fall River, Massachusetts. My senior year of college, I decided I needed more health-care experience. So I accepted a position as the orderly in the emergency room at Union Hospital. Outside of the intensive care units, the only emergency cart was in the Emergency Room. My job was to roll this large cart with EKG machine, breathing tubes, medications, suction, etc., to the place in the hospital where the cardiac emergency is occurring. So one Saturday evening an emergency is called. Unplug this large cart, start rolling down the corridors, into the elevator to the old, original Stephens building patient ward. It was an original part of the hospital and the only lighting in the rooms was plug-in floor lamps. So I arrive with the emergency room doctor, who also was assigned to respond to cardiac codes. My job gets this cart in position and plug in it in so the EKG gets power to turn on. Remember, 1973, not much was battery powered. So where do I plug it in? Oh shit, the only plug is under the bed. The pressure is on, must get this powered on, so therapies can get started. So I get down on my hands and knees and crawl under the bed. Crap again, one outlet, two plugs in, which one do I pull to power the cart? So I pull one, everything goes dark! Now I'm screwed. Under the bed, the room dark, and all you can hear is me tapping the wall with the plug trying to connect the crash cart with the outlet. The doc and nurse grab a battery-powered laryngoscope, which is used to place the breathing tube into the patient's trachea to ventilate and breathe for the patient. Then they hand me, under the bed, the laryngoscope to find the outlet, and voilà! The lights go on and the resuscitation begins. We were successful, the patient survived, but lesson learned. Grab a flashlight for the next emergency.

CHAPTER 8

I eventually graduated from Rhode Island College Nursing program in 1974 and accepted a position as an operating room (OR) nurse at Rhode Island Hospital, Providence, Rhode Island. An interesting side note, I had to lie to my instructors, telling them that I was seeking a position in the emergency room. Because when I was initially seeking letters of recommendation for jobs, my nursing instructors felt that OR nursing wasn't nursing and I should seek a position somewhere else within the hospital that had more hands-on patient care. So in order to meet my needs, I lied to them. I told them I had seen the light of their wisdom and I was applying to other positions within the hospital, either emergency room or intensive care units. Yet when I met with Human Resources, I applied for an OR position. It wasn't until after graduation that they learned I was accepted to the operating room position. Again, that decision, as others I was making, positively steered me to a career that would define my life in so many ways.

My first day in the operating room, I meet my preceptor, Joe Pytel RN. He was the sole male operating room RN. Not having enough lockers for my personnel items and change into OR attire, we shared lockers. Joe was much taller than me, so he had the top shelves, and I was assigned the bottom. Joe was an army Vietnam veteran operating room technician. He spent a year in the war zone, caring for our injured troops. Joe would occasionally throw out tidbits of his time spent in the military and his war experience. In fact, he met his wife in Vietnam, as she was an officer RN, in the army. But now, Joe had a beard, long hair, and swore that he would never ever wear a military uniform again. But fate and life determines changes that are beyond our understanding, as years later Joe and I would be in the same army reserve unit in Massachusetts. Imagine that, Joe had swore he never, ever, over and over again be in an army uniform. But there he was, years later in uniform, doing his 20 years, still serving our Country and the troops, preserving their health. I also met another nurse in the recovery room, Sue Augustus, who would later join the Rhode Island Air National Guard, and later become its Commander. Again, fate is surrounding me, directing me, to a career of service in uniform, all without my knowledge.

I left Rhode Island Hospital 1976 and entered the operating room at Union Hospital. Tricia and I were eventually married in April 1976. At that time, salaries and retirements for nurses were extremely inadequate. I was concerned that I would have difficulty supporting our marriage and future family. Tim Jost and Steve Borden were also working at Union Hospital at this time. Tim and Steve were hospital orderlies during the same time as I was emergency room orderly in 1974. Tim and Steve were both married, having a family to support, so I thought I would run a question by them. I asked Tim, one day after he was brought a preoperative patient to the OR, was he working a second job to raise enough funds to support his family? I will never forget his response, "Eddie, don't get a second job, join the army reserves." What! Yep! He and Steve had low lottery numbers and had joined the reserves much earlier. The Army Reserves were their second part-time income. They were officers in the 399th Combat Support Hospital. Their responsibility was one weekend a month and two weeks' annual training each year. He said, "It's easy, and the monies good without having a bigger commitment working a second job." So Tim had the recruit officer call me to set up a day to visit the unit. Long story short, filled the paperwork out, took my oath of office, and was accepted into the US Army Reserves as a First Lieutenant 1978. So I go to my very first drill weekend, January in uniform. All spit and polish, excited to meet my fellow soldiers. I arrived early and through the main entrance door, a familiar face, although clean-shaven and in uniform. Joe Pytel! The same bearded, sloppy-haired OR nurse at Rhode Island Hospital who had said he would never ever put on another military uniform, Joe Pytel! Again, fate is circling, leading me to an end point, which I still couldn't see clearly.

Tim was right, the reserves were better than getting a second civilian job. I left Union Hospital in the fall of 1977 and entered the Adult Nurse Practitioner program at the University of Rhode Island. The reserves allowed me to study on those drill weekends and at annual training. It was a great part-time job. Basically the reserves paid me to study, one weekend a month and a two-week annual training. During my two years at the university, two more Vietnam veterans joined our unit. Both had Vietnam wartime experience, Dave Foher RN a navy corpsman and Skip Barboza RN, an army medic. Joe, Dave and Skip, obliviously bonded, recapping their experiences in war, while others and I stood silently on the sidelines listening, not having any wartime experience to add to the conversation. As I previously explored, my uncles would relate their wartime experiences in my presence, now my peers were doing the same, with me still on the sidelines. I was in uniform, but still have nothing to offer. I'm in uniform, but still an outsider in this particular military grouping. Forever wondering, how would I respond in these life and death situations within the war zone. Experiencing and dealing with life and death trauma as an operating nurse within the civilian hospital setting, I understood some of the carnage of the human body that could result from trauma. But I wondered how I would not only handle those immediate issues, but how would it affect me coming home. Joe, Dave, Skip seemed to do well, with their job, family, social relationships and then back in uniform. Would I be able to do the same? During this time, I completed my studies at the University, I was an Adult Nurse Practitioner with a Master's Degree. Tricia and I actually talked to an Army recruiter at this time. But both our parents talked us out of a military career at this time. It was post-Vietnam, with all those issues. Looking back, we should have committed to a military career at that time. But we didn't and moved on to another career, not really by choice however.

It was 1979, as a nurse practitioner in Rhode Island. The job as a nurse practitioner was not well defined. Initially, I was unemployed throughout the summer of 1979. I volunteered on the Warren Rescue

Squad and actually delivered a baby on the back of the rescue truck. Finally, a position opened up in Braintree Massachusetts in a sports medical clinic. But the salary was actually less than my OR nursing two years previous. So after a few months, a position was offered to me, at the Brockton Veterans Hospital, supposedly as a NP in the emergency room. Well, it was a disappointment. What actually was happening, without my knowledge was the department of nursing wanted to add a nurse practitioner position to the ER. But they didn't have enough money for a separate NP and RN position. They expected me to do both positions at the same time. So there was a Medical Doctor and a Physician Assistant already assigned to the ER. So it was difficult to oversee the correct disposition of their patients and attempt to utilize my practitioner skills. I was now at a crossroads for my career. Not happy with either positions or not knowing where my future is heading. Tricia and I sat down and examined all our options. Should I go into teaching? Or continue with my nursing career? I enjoyed the OR, felt I could expand my role, and take on a greater responsibility level; I would apply to the nurse anesthetist program. Tricia agreed, let's do it!

I applied to St. Joseph School of Anesthesia for Nurses, in Providence, Rhode Island. All of a sudden, things started to go our way. I was offered a position during my initial interview. I accepted immediately, I felt I was on my way to finally be satisfied with my career choices. This is where I meant Dan McDonald, a classmate who was a Marine Vietnam Vet. Throughout the 30-month program, Dan and I became close. Couple this with my monthly army reserve unit members, my respect for all their service strengthen my commitment to service and Country. With the completion of the program, Dan and I accepted a position at a hospital in Rhode Island. There was another nurse anesthetist, Keith Macsoud, who was in the Army Reserve Unit in Rhode Island. So it started to become evident, that no matter where my life took me, the military would always be a constant. Whether though family, work, social, and professional contact, the common theme was always a military connection somehow. It became quite oblivious about this time that I would be committed, to some degree, to a military career, whether reserves or active duty.

My first job at Miriam Hospital, as a nurse anesthetist out of school I was in Providence, Rhode Island, Tricia and I had our second daughter, Renee. This was an issue though. The last three months of Tricia's pregnancy was one issue after another. I would work all week at my job, on the weekends Tricia would somehow begin premature labor. So into the Hospital, she would go on Friday, get medicated, Renee would calm down in utero and Tricia would be released home on Sunday night. My mother and/or mother-in-law would babysit our first born, Jennifer. Then the next week, it would begin all over again. Then one day, a new doc said that Tricia had a pulmonary blood clot, another issue, but that proved to go nowhere. This kept going on right up to the Thanksgiving holiday. Tricia was doing well so I went to the store to purchase our Thanksgiving groceries. When I returned, my cousin Joan and Tricia were crying. Yep, another weekend of premature labor, or so I thought! So back to the hospital, (Kent County Hospital in Warwick) with Tricia over the holiday weekend we went. But at his time a decision was made to deliver our child. It was thought best at this time to deliver Renee via C-section.

This created another issue however. Renee was six weeks early and had some respiratory issues. So this little premature baby was rushed via ambulance to Providence Woman's' and Infants Hospital intensive care unit. So I was working at Miriam Hospital, Tricia was at Kent County Hospital, and Renee was at the Woman's and Infants Hospital. Tricia wanted to breastfeed our baby, so my life now got even more complicated. I would get up early, take Jen to either my mother's or mother-in-laws, depending on the day, go to Kent County Hospital, get the breast milk, then travel to Woman's and Infants, drop off the milk, say hi to baby Renee, then go to Miriam Hospital to work at my anesthesia position. After work, repeat the whole process over again. When Tricia was released, it saved me a few steps until Renee was released from the intensive care to home. It seemed as if normalcy was beginning, but I was far from right on this aspect too.

Our new daughter had respiratory issues and our rented apartment had mold, which we only discovered by accident. So we had to move quickly to another apartment. But the new apartment, which we didn't know at the time, had an inefficient heating system. Now this was a 1982, and one month heating bill was approximately SEVEN HUNDRED DOLLARS, yep, that's right, seven hundred dollars. Financially we were strapped. There was no way we could continue in this way. I told Tricia, we need to go active duty and she agreed. That very night, I called the Army Nurse Recruiter, and the process to a new career and lifestyle began.

CHAPTER 9

I was told that because I was new to the Army, and with only a year of anesthesia after school under my belt, my first assignment would be to a Medical Center. My first choice was William Beaumont Army Medical Center (WBAMC) in El Paso, Texas, which was granted. I choose WBAMC because of a number of reasons, it was designated a trauma center, neonatal intensive care center, limb re-implantation, obstetrics, and multiple surgical specialties for military, retirees, and civilian patients along with phase two clinical site for the military nurse anesthesia program for the entire southwestern United States. I was assigned to El Paso from 1983 until 1986. There was much independence for my anesthesia practice at WBAMC. The caseload at WBAMC was extensive and easily helped my development as an anesthesia provider for just about any critical case, which was presented to me. This is not a bold statement, but one of confidence gained in order to be a valued contributor in the survival of all types of surgical patients, as a member of the surgical team. I would later appreciate this confidence quietly alone, as I would be continually tested as an anesthesia provider in the war zones of Kosovo and Iraq.

During my time at WBAMC, a number of personal important episodes in our life occurred. Tricia and I had two more children, Rachelle and Jessica, raising our family to four girls. My father-in-law suddenly died during this time, which resulted in our returning to Rhode Island as a family. Later during our time, there my dad had his first open heart surgery, which required my sole return to Rhode Island. Scheduling anesthesia services at WBAMC was a little tight. In fact, with the birth of Jessica, because she was born around 11:30–11:45 PM, I was required to show up for the surgery schedule that next day. I'll never forget. It was an abdominal aortic aneurysm, which after I completed, patient in the ICU and stable, I was allowed to go home and tend to my other 3 girls which one of the neighbors was so kindly taking care of them for us. Financially, the army allowed me to only defer my school loans for three years, but I still was required to fully pay them back after that time. Which I did, by the time I was forty-eight years old, and out of active duty, but it helped, so no complaints.

During one stressful night on in-house call at WBAMC will forever remain in my memory. There was an Indian family from one of the reservations, a family of eleven coming into El Paso to trade in their truck for a newer one. As you can imagine, eleven people in a truck, not everyone had seat belts, and the majority of them were in the rear bed of the truck. Well the worst happened, a drunken driver hit them head on. As the report goes, the people in the back, young and old were propelled like rockets and "there were bodies everywhere." I was the sole anesthesia provider on call, and it was a very long night for me. Some were taken to the civilian hospital, but the most critical were taken to WBAMC, as we were the regional trauma center. We saved a few and lost a few that night. It was devastating. The ones we lost, we had to leave in each operating room, and just move on to the next operating room in an attempt to save the next family member. As morning approached and the regular staff began to arrive for day, it resembled a battle zone. Multiple operating rooms were used, some still had deceased patients in them, as we had moved from one room to another to salvage as many as we could in the shortest amount of time. As I said, we lost some and we saved some, hopefully we all did the best we could.

Going home after that night, as you can imagine, I was spent, exhausted, and emotionally troubled. My wife, Tricia, said she needed to go to the store for some necessities, I said you go, I'm too tired, and I'll watch our girls. So Tricia left, I sat down, still in uniform and directly fell asleep in the chair. The next thing I heard was our phone ringing. Our next-door neighbor, Nancy, asked to talk to Tricia and where is she, which I replied "she was not here, she was out shopping." Nancy then asked who was minding our girls. I was indignant and said I was! Her reply was "Well, your girls were naked and running around the neighborhood!" Well, as you can imagine, I jumped up, rounded the girls and their clothes, and redressed them and didn't rest again until Tricia returned. It was El Paso, in the summer, hot, dry, and the girls I guess didn't feel they needed their clothes. The incident immediately brought me back to a reality after such a stressful and permanent mark in my memory.

After my three years at WBAMC in El Paso, I was reassigned to Cutler Army Hospital at Fort Devens, Massachusetts. Traveling back to New England, one of the stops we made was at West Point, thinking with young kids, breaking up long rides would be easier for them and us. Well, unbeknown to us, it was graduation day at West Point. So many people, but was exciting for my girls was that at the West Point Chapel, there were weddings scheduled every hour. So to keep my four daughters happy and quiet, we would watch multiple bride and grooms exit the Chapel for their pictures before our room was available. Attending the Academy had always been a dream, but never a real opportunity for me. Graduation day, with all its pomp and celebrations, was truly a special time with everyone in their formal dress uniforms; very impressive. After two days, visiting the museums and walking the grounds, it was on to Fort Devens and a new assignment and experiences.

At Fort Devens, I was assigned to Culter Army Community Hospital. Our anesthesia department consisted of three persons, an MD, and two nurse anesthetists, of which I was obliviously one. As nurses, we were pretty much an independent practice, as the MD was off post and we nurses were housed on Fort Devens. As nurse anesthetists we did our own pre, intra, and post operation duties; on call, we were the sole anesthetists available. I thought this would be a more comfortable small community anesthesia practice, especially after leaving all the trauma and high-level cases at William Beaumont. Sadly, my first night on call, I was emergently called to the hospital for a sudden infant death syndrome. We tried valiantly to resuscitate this poor child but to no success. Losing a patient is always difficult, a child there is no comparison, and it never leaves you. These children in their death, their skin takes on a porcelain type sheen, they resemble a beautiful angel.

Fort Devens at the time had the 10th Special Forces assigned there. Due to these highly motivated and special soldiers, there were always injuries and wounds that needed to be surgically repaired. We were busy, but it was rewarding supporting these fighters and their families. Interesting side note, I administered anesthesia to a chopper pilot's son, who was a serve asthmatic for tonsillectomy. The child did well, and I guess the pilot was appreciative. At the time, one of the Secretary of Defense Aids needed to fly into Boston for a meeting. The Aid was to come to Fort Devens, and he would be flown to Boston via military helicopter. The pilot asked if I would accompany them in a chase helicopter for both as the medic and to thank me for the treatment of his son. Of course, I said yes! So at the prescribed time at early evening I was in a Chase helicopter following the Aid. The Aid's Copter landed somewhere in Boston, and we went on a joy ride around the city. We hovered over Fenway Park and watched the Red Sox play for a short while, went by the harbor, Bunker Hill Monument, and the USS Constitution. But a problem arose, FULL BLADDERS! What do we do? Our Pilot said, "No issue," and he made a call. We flew over to the Harvard University football field and landed on the 50-yard line. There were police, fire engines, and red and blue lights all over the place. The copter shut down, we all raced off the field, relieved ourselves, raced back to the chopper, and back into the air. So yes, I have been to Harvard and have been on the field of Glory. Back in the air for a few more hours until the Aid was back at the airport safe, and with no issues except our bodily problems.

Over the two years I was assigned at Devens, a couple of life-changing events happens. First I met Captain Paul Astaphan, also from Rhode Island, whom would later be in my 399th CSH reserve unit and be assigned in Iraq with me, as the Executive Officer. Second I would take on a weekend job Friday and Saturday nights, when not on call at Cutler Army Hospital. My role was as a trauma nurse anesthetist, in house call, at the University of Massachusetts Medical Center, in Worcester, Massachusetts. And thirdly, but probably more significantly, Tricia and I had our 5th daughter, Kary-Anne. We have to thank our neighbors Eddie, a 10th Special Forces Warrant Officer and his wife Lynda. What started out, as a mutual grass-cutting endeavor, ended up as Eddie's adlib Special Forces squad party, strawberry margaritas, and whatever happens after that, is a little foggy. I found out about Tricia's pregnancy of our 5th daughter while I was at UMass Medical center on the weekend. The doc I was with at the time couldn't believe it, 5 kids and they said, "You need to go home now, to be with your wife!" So I left and on the ride home wondering where this was goanna take our family and my career. Lynda, Ed's wife, was so helpful during this time, taking care of our 4 children, while I was at work and on call, as Tricia was again bed redden for the last three months of this pregnancy.

This was the time before 2001 and the Iraq and Afghanistan wars. The military's mandatory assignments were a year unaccompanied in Korea, or two years unaccompanied in Europe, plus six months in Central America. Meaning being assigned at these sites was to be without family. Tricia, with five young girls (one newborn), didn't feel comfortable or wanted to be left alone for all this time. To be honest, we were in agreement; I didn't want to leave my young family during this time either. So the decision was made, I would leave the army, return to Rhode Island and rejoin the Army Reserves, the 399th Combat Support Hospital again. I secured employment at the Miriam Hospital, a teaching hospital associated with Brown Medical School, as a nurse anesthetist, in Providence Rhode Island for a year and a half. Wanting to move on from a teaching hospital, I took a job at Charlton Memorial Hospital in Fall River, Massachusetts.

Again to my surprise, Sue Augustus CRNA was there, who basically I've been following my whole career, and again to my amazement two of the anesthesiologists were Vietnam veterans, Dr. Geremia and Dr. DeFluente, who had served together in Vietnam as anesthesiologists. As they were the anesthesiologists in a combat zone, my friend in the 399th CSH Dave Foher (as I found out later) was a surgical scrub with them in Vietnam. These two docs would share with me their experiences of giving anesthesia in the war zone. Colonel Sue was now in the career status ladder to be Commander of her unit within the Rhode Island Air National Guard. It seemed no matter which direction my path took; the military was guiding me to a direction, which was unknown to me, toward my future in a war zone. While in my time at Charlton Hospital, our unit, 399th CSH received orders to Kosovo in 2001. I was to be the sole nurse anesthetist for the entire 7-month rotation, sharing my anesthesia duties with 3 separate anesthesiologists. Each American anesthesiologist was rotating through a three-month cycle. I was to be the stable anesthesia practitioner throughout the deployment.

CHAPTER 10

There were a few interesting personality issues, which occurred even before we left the tarmac for Kosovo. My sister's husband, LTC Raymond Murray, was the Executive Officer for our deployment. His son, Specialist Raymond Jr. was also deployed with us assigned to the dental section. My good friend Major "Wild" Bill Flanagan was the Pharmacy Officer, who became instrumental and exceedingly vital during our trauma codes. Sadly, two of our closest friends, LTC Brian Campbell CRNA, and Major Mike Nott RN, would not be deployed with us due to mostly political issues with the Chief Nurse, who would later be relieved. LTC Campbell would later be able to join us as an important liaison, using his interpersonally skills, to foster our communication between the civilian hospitals and schools with our NATO hospital. Major Nott became Detachment/Company Commander for the 399th CSH at our base site in Massachusetts, and was instrumental in the plans for our return.

The hospital complex that we, as the 399th CSH, fell in on in Kosovo was a Deployable Medical Systems (DEPMEDS). It was developed in around the 1980s to replace the Mobile Army Surgical Hospitals, formally known as the MASH units. The DEPMEDS units' modules have a rigid aluminum skeletal system covered by heavy rubberized tent like system. These are called Tent, Expandable, Modular, Personnel, or TEMPER units. It has electricity for lights, heating air conditioning, all the comforts of home! These modules are attached to critical van-like containers, called ISO-standard shelters that are expandable for laboratory, radiology, pharmacy, operating rooms, and sterilization departments. But like all tent systems, the air condition works better in the winter and the heating system works better in the summer! But this was our home for the 7 months and we made it work.

With this being my first mobilization as a member of the 399th Combat Support Hospital, we were assigned to Camp Bondsteele, Kosovo, for the time frame February through to October 2001. My formal assignment was as Chief of anesthesia services for the only level three NATO Hospital within Kosovo. During our rotation, we were fortunate to be able to combine the NATO hospitals of the United States and the United Kingdom, a first for NATO. As chief, some of my unique administrate responsibilities were to coordinate this integration of US Army and United Kingdom anesthesiologists into one service, being available for all traumas and routine surgical services. A unique and sometimes politically sensitive administrative development occurred with the integration of our two hospitals. I was a Colonel, by date of rank, outranking both United States and United Kingdom physician anesthesiologists. To complicate the matters even worse, the United Kingdom did not recognize (at least this time) certified registered nurse anesthetists (CRNA), and the independence we enjoy as independent practitioners, especially within our military service. The United States MDs were both comfortable with my independence during their three month rotation and were a great support in reinforcing my independent practice to the United Kingdom docs who also rotated, but in a 4 to 6 week tour. Three USA docs, MAJ Cortella (both he, and a general surgeon, MAJ Cataldo, whom I will be reunited later in another deployment) and COL Lambert were both very supportive in this matter and beneficial to reinforce my independence both in practice and command.

My clinical responsibilities required that I be on first call every other day for 24 hours, responding to all trauma and surgical services as the first provider. Once our hospitals merged, with the United Kingdom, that rotation was every third day. We were always ready for any overflow of cases and Mass Causalities (MassCal's). We handled many severe trauma cases during the busiest time of deployments into Kosovo. MassCal's were a common occurrence and long arduous, stressful hours of attempting to preserve life and limb in the operating theater resulted. Many of these trauma cases were a result of the religious fighting and torturing between the various religious factions. These civilian patients ranged from males of all ages to women and children, which were quite severe and unsettling. The NATO forces injuries were quite destructive, as they were the result of high-powered weapons and explosive devices. Our first causality was a reporter, who was shot and died, as he was being air-lifted to our hospital. The craziness of war was immediately reinforced as we witnessed his pregnant wife accompanying him into our emergency area. So we instantly had two causalities, this reporter and also dealing with his grief-stricken pregnant wife.

Due to my training and position, I served as the primary airway and trauma provider for the transport of the most severe and critically injured American and NATO personnel. This care was provided in a variety of mobile transport units to include Black Hawk helicopters and ground ambulances to the Air Force transport site in Macedonia for a higher-level health care for evacuation to Landstuhl Medical Center (AMC) in Germany. In fact, due to some of the severity of the injuries, at times, I was called upon to accompany the causality to Landstuhl AMC, making independent life-saving decisions in flight. This included at times, airway, fluid and blood replacement, cardiac and neuro-brain stabilization. Seven months of living and working in a stressful situation, you tend to rely on certain people and you tend to think along the same lines in an emergency situation. This was demonstrated during one of our MassCal's. A MassCal is described as more causalities exceeding your available resources. We were overloaded with causalities, very serious ones. We didn't have enough anesthesia and airway support at this critical time. Major Flanagan, the pharmacist, and I were in the emergency area tending to the traumas. At the same time, we both reached for our radios and summoned Lt. Colonel Brian Campbell to the trauma area, as he was in another area at the time. There we were up to our asses in causalities, looked at each other and smiled, as Lt. Campbell arrived answering our simultaneous call. Instances like that happened more than once, but that was the first and became more common during our deployments.

Additional responsibilities include weekly going outside the compound, which we called outside the wire. This included hospitals and clinics within Kosovo. We provided health care to the citizens and education to the health providers. On the road, we were always mindful and vigilant for roadside mines and ambushes. In fact, at one of our sites, we had to abandon our mission because with our initial security survey we discovered two backpacks of explosions. Another time, prior to President Bush and his wife arriving in Kosovo, I was assigned with a limited surgical team to Macedonia to set up a forward surgical team. There were some surgical strikes made by the Macedonia Air Force during this time as well as uprisings at the embassy, which we supported.

Back at home, some significant family issues arose during this time I was in Kosovo, which my wife had to handle alone. As I have stated previously, we have five wonderful daughters. One of them was being treated poorly and bullied by her "friends" at school. She was the focus of many of her peer's comments and harsh remarks. At a special year-end dance, she was in the girl's room and heard some especially crude remarks and took an overdose of Motrin. She had enough presence of mind to report this to a teacher at the dance who appropriately called the rescue department and transported her to the hospital. From that point on, my wife sort professional health care for her. If that wasn't enough, while I was deployed, a different daughter attended Scholar Athletic games during the summer. On one of the social nights, she was raped. She didn't report this to anyone at the time. She tried to keep this hidden from my wife, but issues arose as soon as she returned home. These issues came to full head with family arguments and physical fights between our daughters. My wife, dealing with these issues alone, turned to the rescue squad to transport our daughter to the hospital emergency room. It was there that she revealed she was raped, which came to a shock to us all. She was transported to a special unit where she received support from health providers and family. Through all this my wife had to endure the various testing, i.e., pregnancy, HIV, and hepatitis, which thankfully were all negative. My daughters' names and which number they were in our family have been omitted purposefully to protect them from further and unkind comments. In addition to all this, two of my aunts, Aunt Caroline DeSpirtio (my godmother) and Aunt Jeanne Squillante passed away. These were issues that were difficult to deal with from a distance, knowing that my wife was alone throughout all this turmoil. So upon my return, my energies were directed in attempting to assist my wife in resolving these immediate family issues.

CHAPTER 11

Returning home and back at work at Charlton Hospital, work issues arose, which I was not comfortable with and I decided in 2002 to transfer to St. Anne's Hospital in Fall River, Massachusetts. And to my surprise, the military again was very prominent in the anesthesia department. Again, Sue Augustus CRNA was there, and she was now a Bird Colonel and Commander of her unit, along with Ray Studervant CRNA, veteran of Vietnam who was still in the 399th CSH Reserve Unit. The Chief of the department was Dr. Allison Gorski with Dr. Mary Sippell, a staff anesthesiologist. Both were army-trained anesthesiologists who served together in Hawaii and later served at various military posts. A special mention to Dr. William Guptill, though never in the service was very supportive of the military and my independent nurse practice. When Dr. Gorski hired me, she knew I was committed to the military and that it was after the 9/11 terrorist attacks, in which there was a great possibility I could get activated for an extended period. But as I said, she was military minded, having served herself, and didn't consider it an issue, and in fact was very supportive.

My second deployment occurred in 2003. Although I was a drilling member of the 399th CSH reserve unit, but I was cross-leveled to the 912th Forward Surgical Team (FST) for this deployment. I was notified on a Tuesday and by Thursday of that same week in February, we of the 912th FST were on a bus to Fort Dix, New Jersey, for pre-mobilization training and deployment to Iraq. It was three months of a wide variety of training. Of course, it included military skills training at Fort Dix, but it also included the Army Trauma Training Center at the Ryder Trauma Center, University of Miami, Florida, where we were the lead health care providers for all incoming trauma. At Fort Hood, Texas, we were exposed to Medevac (medical helicopter evacuation) training, "packaging" patients for air transport to the higher echelon hospitals for more definitive care. The Forward Surgical Teams concept (FST) is a small, normally staffed with twenty members. Usually four surgeons, three registered nurses (one each for the emergency room, operating room and intensive care unit), two certified registered nurse anesthetists (CRNA), one administrative officer, one sergeant, three licensed practical nurse, three surgical technicians, and three medics. As a twenty-person mobile surgical unit, we were responsible for salvaging life and limb of critical wounds within the first golden hour of injury. Once the wounds were stabilized, transport of these critical patients is accelerated to the next higher echelon treatment facility, usually within one hour after being released from our surgery. At times, we were able to get our patients directly from our ending of surgery to medevac support for evacuation to the higher hospital or in extreme situations directly from the emergency (mostly severe head wounds) room area. I was responsible for many of these Medevac (helicopter) transports, as these critical patients needed ventilator/airway support, blood pressure maintenance, and fluid and blood resuscitation in-flight. Of the 4 surgeons, in the 912th, I was reunited with Dr. Cataldo, a colorectal surgeon from my Kosovo days. The other surgeon was an orthopedic Dr. Feldman and a pediatric trauma surgeon Dr. Danielson. Together, we were known as the four musketeers.

Our initial stop overseas, we were stationed in Kuwait for a couple weeks, preparing for our assignment with the 1st Armored Division (AD) and watching the burn pit daily. This was the land of three-minute showers, meals ready to eat (MRE's), and sharing a tent with sixty other FST male and female soldiers. We eventually received orders and began our convoy from Kuwait through Iraq. But we had two incidents, which slowed our progress. The first was one of our Humvees broke down with a flat tire and other mechanical issues and had to be eventually towed by one of our other Humvee vehicles. In this instance, we had to take up defensive positions to support and defend those repairing and securing the Humvee to continue the convoy. Guarding the area, we were approached by an unmarked car with a couple of middle-aged men slowing down and pointing at us. I remember pointing my M-16 at them and waving them through and directing them not to stop. They did not stop and slowly passed us, with no incident. The second was a little more serious. We had to bed down in the desert and take security positions throughout the night, after the entire convoy was forced to stop because we were lost in the An Nasiriyan desert area. This was the same area that a similar convoy was lost and came under attack and lives were lost and others taken prisoners.

Once we arrived, our operational area was the Baghdad International Airport (BIAP) area, supporting the 1st AD. We over took a medical building within the missile school on BIAP. Sadam had placed young children schools in his military posts, knowing that we, as Americans, would not target these places with our air superiority with children at the site. The building was in great disarray, and it took a great deal of physical labor of our FST to ready the building for emergency triage and surgical intervention. As the part of the professional medical staff, the doctors and myself were located in a small room together. We were lucky enough to acquire another male surgeon about halfway through our rotation and he was added to our small room. We would comment often, that we knew how "veal" felt. As this building was now where we slept, ate, worked, and took care of our physiological needs, all in this one area. Once we were ready to receive casualties, they were of the most severe sort. Multiple gunshots, mostly to the head region were the most common high-powered injury. But the injuries that were the absolute most common were the IEDs and RPG type injuries. These caused the damage and horrific type of injuries to deal with, both from a visual and clinical aspect.

Attempting to save these people's lives was a common, daily occurrence upon a seemingly never-ending tide of causalities, occurring at all hours. I was called upon more frequently to administer anesthesia as the other CRNA was the commander and she was called upon for administrative duties often. So I became the sole practitioner of anesthesia more frequently than not on a 24-hour basis. Communication was not to be trusted. Injuries, all types of trauma, and multiple patients would be delivered at our doorstep without any notice. We would be summoned at an instant to some sort of human carnage and catastrophe routinely. Another issue with this with this war was the frequency of women being injured. This was a new development, the severe injuries of American female soldiers. Our female soldiers were assigned within the exact same combat area and incurring the same type of grave injuries on a regular basis as our male soldiers. Since I was the father of five (5!) daughters, this affected me greatly. In addition to our military, we provided emergency care, at the same high level, to the civilian men, women, and children who experienced the same devastating injuries and required the same level of life saving surgery. In fact, as providers of equal health care to all, we provided the same high quality of care to the very terrorists who created the bloodshed and butchery, which we attempted to correct with our health care skills.

As in Kosovo, I was the primary provider of care for the transport of the most seriously injured patients from BIAP to our higher echelon Combat Support Hospital. In the beginning, I was able to transport our patients by ground ambulance. Later on due to the fact that the ground ambulances were targeted by terrorists' IEDs, RPGs, and snipers, it was directed by higher command that all our patients would be transported by air ambulance, regardless of severity. As the provider of choice, I was able to monitor, revive, and resuscitate in route these critical patients. Most of patients were transported to the next higher echelon of health care to the 28th Combat Support Hospital. During our time at BIAP, our supplies became critically low. I volunteered to convoy by ground on a couple occasions through unfriendly areas and secured much needed surgical supplies from the 28th CSH and other Forward Surgical Teams (FST) that were being redeployed homeland ahead of us.

We were without any type of communication to family, friends for about six weeks, meaning that there was no snail mail, email, or telephone calls available. We were the medical support within our area for Task Force 20, Seal Team 5, 5th Special Forces Group, and the FBI Hostage Rescue Team. The FBI team, in appreciation of our services to both them and their "patients," allowed each member of the 912th FST to use their telephone services to call home once a week for 15 minutes. Until we were able receive mail, this was our only interaction with our loved ones at home. A surprising follow-up note, the 804th RSC did give our commander a satellite phone, but she used it for her sole purpose, early on, saying it was to be used only for official business. As issues were later raised by our unit with the 804th, she opened it up to the members of the 912th FST.

We were stationed at the edge of the perimeter of the compound at BIAP. Our area was mortared multiple times by the opposing forces. One particular incident occurred on July 19, 2003, there was mortar and small-arms firing, the enemy actually breached our perimeter. As the quick reactionary force was called into action, we had to take fighting positions within our treatment facility. My position was guarding the front door of the clinic with my M-16, preparing for triage and treatment of causalities as well as protecting the patients in the holding area of Charley Company, 47th Forward Support Battalion that was attached to us on BIAP. Our total 912th FST unit was awarded the Combat Action Badge for this particular action.

Toward the end of my tour with the 912th FST, I received news that my number two daughter's fiancé, John Michael Silvia, had died in a single car accident. He was driving home from seeing my daughter late at night after leaving his summer employment as a cook in a local restaurant. Both he and my daughter were planning on asking my permission to marry upon my return from Iraq. Because we were only able to call home once a week from the FBI, this message was given to me by one of the returning 912th FST members from his once a week call. My daughter was obliviously distraught and required much support and counseling from family members and our parish priest Father Marcello. I owe him much thanks, our parish priest was there when I wasn't. The kindness extended during this time, by all the members of the 912th FST, was demonstrated by them all surrendering their weekly 15-minute calls home to me, so that I could call daily home. This was so that I may share in the grief and stay in contact with my daughter and family during this time.

Their kindness was very much appreciated, but I had enormous guilt that I had taken their time from communicating with their families.

When I returned home, my wife and I dealt with this issue of death of my daughter's boyfriend, and the older issue, the daughter that was raped earlier, and the one that had taken the overdose at her high school dance. The daughter that was raped and a girlfriend attempted to run away from home. They were both found and brought to hospitals where their issues were treated with hospital inpatient admissions. A happy note to my daughter who lost her fiancé, after counseling and much support, got married in 2008 to a wonderful boy, Andrew Turenne, who was sensitive to her issues. But it has been a difficult ride to this point with these three daughters to normalcy.

Arriving home, I developed an issue that has been part of my being and has only gotten worse and developed to a greater extent and added too, with another future deployment. I developed a startle response to sudden and unexpected loud noises. This was exhibited the very first week I was home. One of my daughters was a lifeguard at the town beach. At the end of the day, she was responsible to place everything into the shed at the beach. I went to pick her up in our family car. After placing everything in, she slammed the shed door, creating a load shattering noise. I jumped out of the car and hit the ground. She was startled. My excuse was I was looking for the car keys, even though the car was still running! And the keys were in the car! Since that time, and after my future deployment, my family and coworkers have had to deal with this idiosyncrasy of my personality, my startle response. Dr. Gorski and my fellow workers at St. Anne's welcomed me home, all believing, including myself, that 2003 was my last deployment.

CHAPTER 12

But that deployment in 2003 was not to be! I was ordered to my third deployment with our reserve unit, the 399th Combat Support Hospital for 2006–2007. This deployment was for over 17 months to include our training at Fort McCoy. My very first day of deployment started with an issue. It was the same day as my fifth daughter graduated from Mount Hope High School from Bristol Rhode Island on 07 June 2006. This daughter was Vice President of her senior class and President of the Student Council. She would be given two speeches at graduation. I was granted permission and was allowed to witness her graduation, but had to leave directly after to show up to our pre-deployment mobilization station, not able to attend her graduation party. It was a lonely sober ride to my drop-off site with my wife, daughters, and a few of their boyfriends. We shared a foreboding feeling, and we all knew of all the issues that have occurred with the previous deployments. It was a about a three-month training cycle at Fort McCoy, this included a trauma course at Fort Sam Houston, Texas, with experiences on cadavers learning emergency life-saving procedures.

As in the past, another issue presented itself early during my deployment phase. My oldest daughter was to be married in August 2007. Because the 399th CSH was scheduled to leave Iraq in the September/October 2007 time frame, higher headquarters (3rd MEDCOM) did not want to schedule any routine leaves within the 2–3 month end of tour. In order to gain permission to attend my daughter's wedding, I had to forgo leave between Fort McCoy and deployment to Iraq, which everyone else was given 6 days, to be with their families prior to deployment. I would also have to volunteer to be the Advance Party Commander (ADVON) to Kuwait, and prepare for the arrival of the entire 399th CSH arrival in Kuwait and to go over the "berm" into Iraq. So in agreeing to that, I would have to forfeit the 6 days awarded to everyone within the 399th CSH after completing training at Fort McCoy. As a result, it would be a full 17 months until I would see my family again in order to be present for my daughter's wedding in August 2007. I agreed to this without hesitation, as I most definitely wanted to walk my firstborn down the aisle.

Once the entire hospital was in place in Kuwait, orders were that we were to be in a split operation. As the hospital was split in two, the sites were identified as Tirkit and Mosul, Iraq. I was once again designated as the chief of anesthesia at the Mosul site. Most of my clinical friends and support systems that I had developed over the years within the 399th CSH were to be assigned at the Tirkit site. Although I did have some support systems, i.e., friends in the administration headquarters, my closest friends within the hospital setting were assigned to the Tirkit site, LTC Mike Nott, COL Brian Campbell and COL Quick. I was lucky enough that two of my friends were assigned with me in Mosul, but they were within the administration section, COL Paul Astaphan and LTC Mike Kolodziel. Due to our different assignments within the hospital however, I would only be able to see these two at supper, maybe 4–5 times per week. This would be because of some of their administrative commitments verses my responsibility to the surgical patients. As before, the operating room was a 24-hour responsibility responding to surgical crisis for multiple traumas and mass causalities. Because of my rank and position within the anesthesia and operating room staffs, there was a level of military separation between the staff and myself. It became very lonely over the year, not having the associations that I had earlier during my reserve career back home.

From the very first day that the hospital was handed over to the 399th CSH in Mosul, from the preceding unit, we experienced a mortar attack, followed by a mass causality. Patients were overflowing and exceeding our resources. We were equipped to have three surgical procedures simultaneously with our three surgical beds. Two surgical beds were in one room and a third was in our depmeds surgical container. However, from that first day, due to the large number of causalities we would receive, I would direct anesthesia services in the operating room, emergency room, intensive care unit, and CT scan simultaneously. Running from each area directing the CRNAS's, nurses, respiratory therapists, and medics, accounting for ventilator support, pain medication, blood transfusions, and drugs for blood pressure support and cardiac stability. This would be a common thread while we were in the Mosul site. In fact, the Boston Globe photographed me directing anesthesia and resuscitation for a critical patient in the intensive care unit during one of these Mass Cals exceeding our surgical suite capabilities, which was displayed on their front page December 31, 2006.

Our time in Mosul it was commonplace for multiple serve injuries and services that were stretched to the limits of our resources, which we dealt with on a regular basis. There were gunshot wounds from high-powered weapons, but the majority of patients had wounds from IEDs and RPGs. These were ghastly and horrific wounds. These patients required massive blood replacement and multiple procedures to stabilize patients. We took care of everyone, soldiers, civilian, children, and the terrorists themselves. They all received the highest standard of care, and the most critical patients, no matter what their status, were our first priority.

Dealing with death, dismemberment, massive blood replacement, and pain were commonplace in our normal interaction with patients. These issues were part of our normalcy within this war environment. Severely burn patients and central nervous system injury patients were so challenging, that at times nothing could be done for them medically, excepting comfort measures in order to let them die peacefully as we comforted them, with a held hand, pat on their head, and a prayer. Body parts were often brought in with patients, being separated by the explosion. Amputating arms and legs routinely with just bandage scissors in the emergency room was not uncommon as the injuries were so severe that only a small amount of tissue would remain connected to the patient's limbs. Tourniquets were applied to severed and mangled body parts to prevent exsanguination of the patient. Multiple limbs of individual patients being decimated by explosions and then dealing with the results of the trauma, as these multiple limbs were lost became commonplace. The debris from the explosions would have to be removed from these patients. It could include just about anything, dirt, steel ball bearings, various metals, and even the very bones of the terrorist.

After you would be exhausted from the hours in the operating room saving these lives, especially our American troops, then you would wonder about the life these young people will have to endure with such extreme injuries. Then there were those with open abdominal wounds and internal contents lay open on their chest. People (our troops, civilians, terrorist, and children) would arrive to our hospital almost severed in half, and it was our task to repair them. We often asked each other, how do you become immune to these sounds, sights, and smells, day after day, and night after night, over and over again? Patients pleading to us with their eyes and screams through every kind of emotion, in hopes we could administer aid to prevent pain or to save their life or limbs. Dealing with a loss was never easy or accepted. We saved many patients. But the ones you remember, the ones that stay with you, are the ones you lose. Those are the ones that keep you up at night, these are the memories that never go away. We lost patients from lack of blood replacement, bleeding that could not be controlled, even as we attempted to do whole blood drives from our ranks.

As mentioned before, we administered care to all who arrived though our doors, to include the very terrorists who attempted to take our lives and those of our allies. This included children who were directed by their parents to place IEDs in the roadside and these IEDs were mistakenly exploded premature causing injury to these young children while implanting them. The image of amputating a child's hand or leg is not an image you can soon forget. Mass causalities were frequent: we had at least 12–15 of them. This included the time about 12 wounded children were emergently brought in because a terrorist bombed a child's soccer game. I hated holidays; to this day, holidays still are bittersweet. The terrorist seemed to arrange their biggest campaigns against us when we celebrated our special times. The day after Thanksgiving, Christmas Day, Mother's Day, and others will forever be ingrained into my very being with the horror of us frantically piecing together and saving broken individuals who were horribly blown up and mangled. Our holidays were long and joyless, petrified and tattooed by the realities of war. The operating room at the end of surgery covered in bright red bloody fluid was always a stark contrast to the blue surgical drapes. It was a visual reminder that there was a battle here in the operating room, a battle to fight death. Most times, we won, but the result was costly, to both patient and to us.

Christmas for me will always be a bittersweet celebration. Tricia had sent wrapped gifts for me, and I placed them under my bunk to be opened on Christmas day. But Christmas was not to be a peaceful day for me. I assigned myself first anesthesia call, to give my staff some holiday time off, if possible. On Christmas morning, I was awoken with an emergency call to the operating room, no breakfast. Finishing with surgery around midday, my dear friend, Lt. Col Cortella MD, and I volunteered to do guard duty at the front door of our hospital. All the officers within the hospital would volunteer on holidays to do guard duty to free up some time for our enlisted folks. During our time at the front door, a three-star general and his entourage arrived. We had them clear their weapons prior to entering. In truth, one had the red dot exposed, meaning ready to fire! This raised some eyebrows, but the general was impressed and he awarded us with a coin for our duty. As soon as I finished our four-hour guard duty, I was again summoned to the operating room, and again, no lunch this time. Finishing with those surgeries, I decided to grab some supper and head over to my bunk and open my gifts. At supper, I was again directed that incoming causalities were arriving and I was needed in surgery. I finished sometime in the early morning, headed over to my bunk, and collapsed. I didn't open my gifts until the day after Christmas. I'd like to take a moment here to explain that at times, those minutes entered into hours and hours entered into days without or very little sleep. There were at times after days of surgery with little or no sleep I would try to rest. Instead, I would hallucinate or relive these injuries. The only thing that calmed me down, allowed me to grab some sleep and rest, would be to recite the Holy Rosary. It was something my wife taught me and helped me numerous times

In Mosul, our general area was mortared over 160 times as verified by the 399th CSH daily log. On the morning of November 6, 2006, there was a mortar attack of about 5 rounds. God was with us. There was one unexploded round that struck within twenty feet of the bunker I was in with others, crashing through one of our living areas. One of the rounds hit the operating room roof, which did explode. Luckily no one was injured.

In Mosul 2006, one of my greatest nonsurgical anxiety occurred. Previously, prior to deployment, I had taken classes for preparation to provide Catholic services in the advent there was no religious person available. I never really thought that I would be called. The priest we had in Mosul was to be away for 3 weeks. He asked at each week at services for someone to step forward. Each week, no one volunteered, and I kept hoping someone, anyone, would volunteer. No one did. At the last week before our priest was to leave, no one had volunteered as yet. So I approached our priest at the last week of services and said I would volunteer as I had had the classes. His response was "I knew God would send someone." When I heard that all I could think of was *Great, what have I done.* How could I do this in front of everyone? I'm not prepared and not worthy and certainly no angel, to lead this congregation of service members through the whole base who will attend. But somehow I was able to do the service give the homily, that the priest prepared for me and administer Holy Communion. Truthfully, I was frightened leading this service. I felt that, who am I? A sinner with so many faults leading this service. Those in attendance thanked me after the 3 weeks of services. I guess in that time, in that place, I was called to serve in a different way and was given the strength and courage. I know it wasn't from my will alone: I had help from the Big Guy, our Lord and Savior! He gave me the strength and stamina to meet this challenge and then more of His strength for the difficult days to follow.

CHAPTER 13

Around January–February 2007, we were ordered by higher headquarters to turn our hospital over to a section of the 28th CSH. We were then given orders to move in total to the western section of Iraq and build from scratch, ground up, a Level III hospital facility in the Al Asad area of Iraq. We were to replace a Navy Level II facility, which is similar to the Army's FST. I was solely responsible for the anesthesia services for this new complex. We completed this facility in record time and within budget. We took great pride in that we, as a reserve unit, were given this order, and completed this mission, a first in the Iraq war.

Once the hospital was completed, we began to again receive these appalling, gruesome, and sickening causalities of war. I don't believe I need to explain again the trauma and destruction to the physical, emotional, and psychological effects these injuries brought to patients and us again and again. It was a never-ending tide of war wounds, countless hours of frantic care, broken sleep, trepidation that there was something more you could do for these patients and exhaustion from the fear that this would not end and we would forever be in this place.

Well, I was finally granted permission to attend my daughter Jennifer's wedding near the end of our tour in 2007. But it was not without issue. It was during the surge into Iraq, which was orchestrated by General Petrus. Also at this same time, an advance party from the hospital unit that was to replace us came in with a small group of soldiers. The officer in charge of this group was a Lt. Colonel. Well, because of the surge, I was denied air transportation for two days, and there was no guarantee of when I would be allowed transportation home. The main focus of the surge was "beans and bullets" and certainly not my daughter's wedding. My daughter was getting anxious and threatened to postpone the wedding if I didn't make it on time. Obliviously, that was a no-go on my account. I directed my wife that it was stupid and just go ahead without me, if I was unable to get transportation home. But there was a window of opportunity on the third day of my trying to get out of country and make it to my daughter's wedding. The advance party of the incoming unit was leaving, and they had reserved seats on the military plane leaving. As I said, the officer in charge of the advance party was a Lt. Colonel, I was a full Colonel, so I just jumped in and declared that I was the Officer in charge of this advance party and I was to leave with them on their next flight. The Lt. Colonel didn't say a word, his eyes were a little bug-eyed though, and I was able to get on the flight and make it to my daughter's wedding on tine. Walking her down the aisle in my full dress uniform, sword and all. Damn, I looked beautiful! After the two-week leave, I returned to Iraq without issue.

There was an issue getting dressed upon my arrival home. For almost seventeen months, all I ever wore was the military uniform. Always the same underwear, socks, boots, and outer uniform, never allowed to venture beyond what was ordered and the required uniform. The first morning home, rising from bed, I went to my dresser opened the door and froze. So many colors, so many options. I honestly didn't know what to choose. My wife asked what was the matter, and I replied I didn't know what to choose. Her sympathetic tone, "Just pick something and put it on." Well, I did, and then her second sympathetic replay, "It doesn't match, pick something else." I did and each day home became a little easier to pick and match my wardrobe.

But as always, with every other deployment I was on, serious family issues arose. My dad became gravely ill, and it was reported that he was dying. Family notified the Red Cross and I was allowed to go home to be with my dad and family at the very end of our deployment. Our unit at the time was planning its re-deployment return to the States with the replacing unit arrival already in place in Iraq. Even in these difficult situations, there are instances where you can feel God or some higher power giving you strength to make it through the hardest times. There was a small interaction with Dad that I will never forget, and that has given me strength and pride to this day.

While I was home on this emergency leave, I received a phone call from my ma that Dad wasn't doing well and that I should arrive to the hospital as soon as possible. There was a miscommunication though. His doctor wanted us, the family, to meet him at his office to discuss end-of-life decisions. In my misunderstanding, I rushed to Dad's hospital bed. I hurried to his intensive care room, arriving there I saw him sitting up, exhausted but watching television. I asked him how he was doing and he mumbled, something like "Fine, but tired." Then he said something I will never forget but treasure. He said, "Eddie, you made my name strong." I was overcome with emotion, and tears started to well up and I could hardly speak. I told him I loved him and that he taught me how to be a man, how to be strong, to protect my wife and kids, and that to sacrifice for family is not a sacrifice at all. I will never forget his words and how proud he made me feel that day. Those words still resonate with me and bring an emotion of pride and sadness. This man, with no more than an eight-grade education, was able in a few simple words to bring true meaning to my life. It was an unexpected honor to know that my dad approved of my life and was proud of the man I had become. Dad died and I was fortunate enough to be able to attend his funeral, and I proudly served as a pallbearer for his casket. Each deployment has had significant personnel loses and issues; this time I lost my father, someone who truly understood my military commitment and duty. He never questioned my deployments, only that I wore the uniform and had a job to do. Dad always told me he was a private first class with a chuckle. But finished that statement by saying he still outranked me, which was never questioned by me. He still outranks me and always will!

Returning from war my last time, I understood that war is the great equalizer of equality. The IEDs, mortars, missiles, bullets, rockets have no memory, no consciousness, and no morals. These instruments of war are indiscriminate in their destructive force. In the War on Terror, there is no forward edge of battle, the battle surrounds you, and it is everywhere. All are equally susceptible to their appalling effects, to include our sisters in uniform. This was a new development of this War on Terror, the severe injuries of our fellow females in uniform. The American female service members are assigned within the same combat area performing tasks that at one time were labeled "male only." These fellow sisters in uniform experienced the same devastating injuries and required the same level of life-saving surgery as any defender of freedom. Since I was the proud father of five wonderful daughters, this affected me greatly. The level of patriotism and professionalism displayed by our female contingent was truly inspirational, and I was proud to stand equally among them.

I am quite proud of my daughters. All of my five daughters have been successful, mostly through their own hard work and dedication. Two have joined the military. My third daughter Rachelle is a captain in the Connecticut National Guard as an Engineer. She has recently returned from a year deployment from Afghanistan (2018–2019) and awarded the MSM medal. My forth daughter, Jessica is a major in the US Air Force, stationed in San Antonio, Texas, as a Social Worker, counseling families, personnel with their various issues of airmen and their families. Jessica's husband, Mark, was a US Marine Sargent, who had multiple tours in Iraq, during some of the most critical times, serving in some of the most dangerous places. Jennifer, daughter number one, is a master's prepared guidance counselor in a high school in Massachusetts, her husband, Jay, is an Environmental Engineer. Renee, daughter number two, is a master's prepared elementary school teacher in Connecticut, and her husband Andrew is a professional fire fighter, master's level prepared. My last daughter, Kary-Anne, is a master's prepared Senior Athletic Trainer in a large Myrtle Beach high school. My wife and I are the proud grandparents of eleven grandchildren.

CHAPTER 14

Coming home for us was markedly different than our Vietnam brothers and sisters. Truly remarkable was the act of selfless patriotism that our Nam brothers and sisters demonstrated later in life in our homecoming. Collectively they vowed to never again allow those who go in harm's way to ever again be denied the honor of service to our country to go unrecognized. They worked unselfishly, along with veterans of other eras toward the goal, that we, who served following them, would never be met with an attitude of ungraciousness or malice as they were. These veterans have collectively worked to an end, that as we arrived home from battle, we were met as champions from a welcoming nation, for service, not victims of political policies.

Upon returning home, I had to spend some time within the Warrior Transition Unit (WTU). I had worn out my knees, a fifty plus year old man trying to keep pace with twenty-year olds. In and out of helicopters, carrying stretchers, transporting casualties by air and ground ambulances, walking miles in the desert sand with heavy packs, most times over fifty pounds, torn me down. I required total knee surgery twice on my left knee during my one-year time in the WTU. I developed a complication called patella clunk syndrome. This syndrome restricted my mobility, with flexion and extension along with being extremely painful. During this time, I was contacted that I might be deployed once again. Because of my limitations and not being able to function at an optimal level, I was referred to a medical board for fitness to return to duty.

The medical board was held at the Walter Reed Army Medical Center in Washington, DC. It was determined that I was unable to return to duty and was medically boarded out of military service. They said I could no longer do field work or care for the causalities in helicopters and land vehicles. As I left the medical board and entered the elevator, I began to cry. This was not the way I had wanted or envisioned my retiring from service.

But my time at Walter Reed answered and gave me hope that I was part of a grouping, which made a difference in this world, for the better. Many times attempting to salvage a human life during my deployments you wonder are you really making a difference. Was I really helping these young men and women with such tremendous, devastating injuries going back into society, and what kind of life would they lead. Well, by God's good graces, I was able to receive the answer. I was actually able to see some of the soldiers which I was part of their surgical care in Iraq. They were in wheelchairs, prosthetic legs and arms, or shuffling and dragging lifeless limbs, but they were with their families. They were laughing, almost joyous, celebrating their future life with their loved ones. Their children and loved ones were not dwelling on their limitations, but on the fact that they were alive, being a part of their future. God had given me a gift, not just my doing a job. God had shown me, I had made a difference to a small group of injured and affected families and their futures in a positive way. I never introduced myself to these soldiers or their families; I just admired them from afar. They would not remember me, as I was the one, which kept them asleep and alive through their surgeries. I silently prayed for them and a thankful prayer to God for showing me that the difference, worth going to herculean efforts to save these soldiers, which I questioned, was answered.

Over the following years, I required three more operations on my left knee and one on my right knee. Returning to my civilian employment at St. Anne's Hospital in Fall River Massachusetts after a year in the WTU, I was met with my army buddies, Dr. Gorski, Dr. Sipplel, and my old nurse anesthetist buddy Sue Augustus, plus a new doc, who was deployed with the Air Force to Iraq, Dr. Korzeniowski, as well as my orthopedic doctor, Dr. Smith who was in the Navy (GO Army, Beat Navy). As was my history, I was comfortable, surrounded by military persons, understanding the sacrifice that was made by wearing the uniform. But my professional story doesn't end here. St. Anne's anesthesia section was sold by the hospital to a larger anesthesia conglomerate, and our section was broken apart.

Looking north and getting ready to retire in a few short years, New Hampshire seemed as an ideal place to set up new roots, no sales tax, no income tax, didn't tax my social security, or my military pay, and was more conservative. So I applied to the Anesthesia Care Group at the Catholic Memorial Hospital. Dr. DelGiudice, the chief anesthesiologist, hired me, and I felt he was generally appreciative of my years of military service. Upon being hired, I was again surprised by the military connection I would be bonded with and would come to appreciate. Dr. Wagner, whose father was a pilot in World War II, Dr. Dennis Kelly, whose father was a retired Marine Sargent, Barry Perlow, ex-army, my PCP Dr. Michaud (Air Force), Brian Nawoj CRNA (Air Force), LTC Tim Schneider CRNA (Desert Storm veteran), my new ortho surgeon, Dr. Gonzales (Desert Storm veteran), CPT Martha Hart and LTC Georgene Vukelich (both military trained CRNA's), the endoscopy chief nurse, Scott Clark and Dr. Poutre, an anesthesiologist and a patriot, who supported me through some of my PTSD issues. As I was winding down my career, it was comforting to be surrounded with others who understood the direction my life had taken. Maybe my military career path was predetermined. Maybe I took the path that was designed for me, or maybe it was the people and what they stood for that I valued the most that affected my decisions. Or maybe it was their commitment to country, to service, their sacrifice, the wonderful memories of hardships, which they shared and laughed at, all for something larger than life itself—our freedoms. That this freedom had to be earned by a few, so that all could enjoy its fruits. I realized early on, I wanted to be one of those who would earn that right. I guess I always wanted to belong to that small special group.

I am not without scars from my military service. Upon the return of each deployment issues arose which impacted upon my relationships with my wife, daughters, extended family, friends, and work environment. In a total of approximately six years, I was away on deployment for almost more than three years. The family issues, which occurred in my absence as described earlier, were significant and life-changing events. I had to deal with each of these from a distance during my deployments.

Meanwhile my wife had to deal with these solely by herself with no support from me, her spouse because of our separations. Returning home, I would have to redirect all my energies to help her resolve these serious issues. I missed many family celebrations and holidays. I also missed the ability to grieve with those close to me at the loss of family members. I had to grieve alone, thousands of miles away from family support. Each time I tried to regroup at home, my country called me to action, which I never denied.

My experiences in the war zones were stressful on many fronts; being responsible for mission success, which meant saving life and limb, soldiers general welfare, self-preservation during multiple attacks, health, trauma, and surgical services for all individuals within the war zone, along with the extreme ranges of emotion in response to the horrendous injuries which required my services daily. Since I have returned, I have difficulty sleeping and my startle reflex to loud noises has increased. My wife and children have commented on numerous occasions of my relieving my wartime experiences in my sleep. These are re-treating war causalities, protecting myself during mortar attacks, small-arms fire, and convoying through enemy zones trying to get medical supplies for our FST. As I have said before, the successes you forget, but the ones we lost, there is always the thought, was there something more that could have/should have been done?

At times, my personality has been altered. My loved ones have continually commented on my not having the patience to deal with civilian mundane issues. At times, in the operating room back home, the smell of blood, large traumas, or the burning of flesh by the surgical bovie, would trigger flashbacks. Trying to control these, I felt it was a better to limit myself to outpatient surgery, which Dr. DelGiudice and Dr. Poute allowed me to do. Doing that, extended my career as a nurse anesthetist and helped my mental attitude, which helped to overcome the issues of reclaiming myself within the civilian world.

I'm retired now. But still maintain closeness to a small band of my army buddies. It doesn't matter how long or when we make contact, it could be days or months (never years), but the bond is always there. These are the people I have shared my most terrifying moments of our lives together. Together we have witnessed the horrors of war, which have bonded us into a friendship that has no easy definition. We are not special people or claim to be privileged. We all have come from middle-class parents who have taught us the same common beliefs. To work hard, expect no handouts, understand that service to country is a privilege and an honorable sacrifice. We understand that our country offers us the ability to achieve our goals, but that ability is determined by our individual sacrifices and hard work. Our parents, our uncles and aunts, who survived the terrors of World War II and taught us the importance of our freedoms, instilled in us this pride in America, which we all possess.

We carried on this commitment by the wearing of the uniform, to follow this tradition begun by them. All of us, LTC Nott, MAJ Flanagan, COL Campbell, COL Astaphan, COL Susan Augustus, LTC Foher, Col Quick, COL Murray, SGT Murray JR and SGT LaBranch, when we are together we are like little school girls giggling, laughing remembering our army times, sharing our experiences, good and bad. Somehow we never really remember the incidences the way that they really actually happened. Many times we embellish them. Most often, we laugh at ourselves. When we gather, our spouses leave us in a corner, not entering into our conversions and our kids leave us alone, most times embarrassed for us, never understanding how we have never grown up. But we are home; together we are in our safe space. I, for one, have come full circle; these were the times I remember in my youth, my relatives laughing and exchanging stories about their military careers during WWII. Now we have our war and our stories. I have worn the uniform for 32 years; I wish I could still wear it, never have to take it off. I, and my friends, am "Soldiers for life!" It was a long journey that I gladly took with no regrets.

ABOUT THE AUTHOR

Edward O. Cyr, retired US Army Nurse Corps Colonel, and retired nurse anesthetist.

Growing up in Rhode Island, Eddie graduated from Rhode Island College with a BS in Nursing 1974. After multiple jobs as an operating room nurse, Eddie attended and graduated from the University of Rhode Island (URI) 1978, with a Master's in Nursing and Adult Nurse Practitioner (NP) concentration. During this time at URI, Eddie joined the US Army Reserve Unit, 399th Combat Support Hospital (CSH) in Taunton Massachusetts, which began his military journey. Being disillusioned with his job opportunities as a NP in 1979, he enrolled at St. Joseph's School of Anesthesia for Nurses in Providence, Rhode Island, graduating in 1982. Shortly after graduation, Eddie joined the active duty Army for five years serving at William Beaumont Army Medical Center in El Paso, Texas, and Cutler Army Hospital at Fort Devens. While at Fort Devens, Eddie and his wife, Patricia, had their fifth daughter and requested to return to the 399th CSH reserve unit. He then worked as a civilian staff nurse anesthetist at several hospitals in Rhode Island and Massachusetts, while simultaneously drilling with the 399th CSH. It was during his career in the 399th that Eddie was promoted to "Full Bird" Colonel and deployed three times to various hostile and war zones. In this capacity, within these deployments, Colonel Cyr was at times the Chief of Anesthesia for the 399th CSH, while in Kosovo 2001 and Iraq 2006–07. In 2003, as a member of the 912th Forward Surgical Team, he functioned as one of only two anesthesia providers. Colonel Cyr is now retired from both the military and his civilian anesthesia responsibilities. His family is comprised of his wife, his daughters (two of which are in the military), their husbands, and their eleven grandchildren.

Awarded the:

Legion of Merit, Bronze Star, Meritorious Service Medal, Army Commendation Medal, National Defense Medal with Star, Global War on Terrorism Expeditionary Medal, Iraq Campaign Medal, Kosovo Campaign Medal, NATO Kosovo Medal. Combat Action Badge and the Expert Medical Field Badge, among others.

Authorized:

Army Meritorious Unit Citation, Five Unit Combat Patches